Personality and Education

Psychology and Education

General Editor: Gerald Cortis

Personality and Education

David Fontana

Open Books
London

First published 1977 by Open Books Publishing Ltd
21 Tower Street, London WC2H 9NS

© David Fontana 1977

Hardback: ISBN 0 7291 0087 1

Paperback: ISBN 0 7291 0082 0

Filmset in 10pt Linotron Imprint

Printed by T. & A. Constable Ltd
Hopetoun Street, Edinburgh

Contents

For Elizabeth

Editor's introduction

The topic of personality is one of the central concerns of education. David Fontana's aim is to introduce readers to research carried out by psychologists in this area and to the practical ways in which their insights can assist teachers and other adults who are engaged in the educational process to function more effectively.

The text examines the formative influences on personality from pre-school years through adolescence, together with the ideas of some influential personality theorists. The relations between personality and other mental abilities, such as intelligence, creativity and motivation are succinctly reviewed and the importance of cognitive style as a basic component of an individual's behavioural organisation is stressed. The book concludes with a review of the nature of mental ill-health and its implications for the educational process.

Personality and Education is one of the titles in the *Psychology and Education* series. Though consumer preference does not constitute the sole criterion of selecting topics for course design, such a preference is a demand that both authors and publishers have not usually been able to meet with exactitude, since reliable information about demand has not been readily available until now. The selection of titles in this series was based on the results of an extensive nationwide survey of teachers of educational studies on the staffs of polytechnics and colleges that I carried out in 1973. The five titles represent the areas that teachers in higher education rated as the most essential elements in their actual or proposed courses in the psychological area of education. The authors, who have all had extensive teaching experience themselves, have taken as their principal aim the introduction of important psychological concepts in each area that are relevant to both educational theory and practice. Our purpose has been to write simply and clearly so that key areas are revealed and a framework is provided on which a student can build further knowledge. The framework embraces both new and long-standing concepts, since new knowledge has a relation to time past. The unity in the series arises from the ultimate selection of the five titles (in terms of the highest survey ratings) by the consumers themselves, though each title has been designed to stand on its own. Given the hybrid nature of both psychology and education some minor overlap of topic areas is inevitable and, in many ways, welcome.

References in the text to the work of other writers, e.g. Jones (1975) are provided so that students may be encouraged, where appropriate to follow up the source named. The book or article so quoted will be listed in the References (which also double as a Name Index) at the back of the book.

Gerald Cortis

Introduction

The aim of this book is to discuss those psychological insights into personality that are of most relevance to education. At the end of it, the reader should know something of the origins and development of personality, something of those theories of personality that crop up most frequently in educational discussion, should have a certain familiarity with the most popular devices for measuring personality, and should be able to understand the implications of all these topics for the work of the teacher. Because it is an introductory text, the purpose will be to draw the reader's attention to what is important, rather than to go into these topics in great detail. Personality is such a vast field within psychology that we cannot hope to do more.

Perhaps this is as good a place as any to make one important reservation. Indeed, if we make it now, there won't be the need to go on repeating it throughout the book. That is, that although the psychologist has spent a great deal of time and effort researching into personality over the last half-century or so, he is still very far away from knowing the whole truth about it. Psychologists like to construct theories, and they like to measure things. I hope I shall say enough in this book to show that these activities tell us sufficient about personality to influence profoundly the way in which the teacher thinks about children. But theories and measurements can only take us so far. I may, for example, construct a theory on the meaning of happiness, devise a test to measure its presence in people, and then find that two children get identical scores on my test. But this doesn't mean that their relative degrees of happiness can really be reduced to equal marks on a paper and pencil test. Even if my test is a good one, it still doesn't tell me that the two children will be made equally happy by the same events. Nor does it tell me how happiness *feels* to the children, the extent to which in each case it can stand up to the blows of fate, the extent to which it will change with time, and so on. Teachers, perhaps more than anyone else, know that children are unique. The only way to know a child is, paradoxically enough, to get to know him. Psychology books are aids towards, and not substitutes for, this process.

WHAT IS PERSONALITY?

The teacher is interested in children's personalities for two reasons. Firstly because he is concerned with how children develop as people, that is with how they relate to others and to themselves, how they develop goals and ambitions in life, how they acquire codes of conduct and styles of behaviour, and how they adjust to the inevitable problems and challenges that are part of being human. And secondly, because he is concerned with the way in which these factors influence a child's academic achievement, since we know that this achievement is dependent not just upon such things as intelligence but upon the whole range of personal functioning that the child brings to bear upon the learning task.

Our first problem arises, however, when we come to define personality. Personality is one of those tantalising terms that seems to retreat the further from us the more we try to grasp it. Everybody thinks he knows what the word means, but the effort of expressing this meaning in any generally acceptable form is often beyond him. Psychologists are no exception to this. As long ago as 1937, Allport listed no fewer than fifty attempts by psychologists at definition, and commented that some of them were so all embracing that they included practically everything that interests the psychologist about people — e.g. 'personality is the entire mental organisation of a human being at any stage in his development'.

More recently, psychologists have tried to be more precise by taking personality to include only such things as sentiments, attitudes, complexes and unconscious mechanisms, interests and ideals (Vernon 1975), and have excluded from it cognitive and physical attributes such as intelligence and motor skills. The term 'affective' is sometimes used to distinguish personality variables from cognitive or physical ones, but strictly speaking, this term relates only to those aspects of personality which have to do directly with the emotions.

Having made this distinction between personality and cognitive and physical variables, we now have to admit that the three influence each other so closely that the layman may feel that this distinction has more to do with the psychologist's convenience than with anything else. Psychology is such a vast subject, that it has to be parcelled up into more manageable units, even if the parcelling is somewhat arbitrary. But by separating personality in this way from cognitive factors, it helps us at least to focus attention upon man as a creature of feelings and moods as well as a creature of intelligence. It helps us to emphasise that he is a social creature, with characteristic ways of reacting to others and towards himself, a creature of beliefs, aspirations and dreams, a creature ruled, as the ancients had it, by the heart as well as by the head.

One of the most satisfactory current attempts to define personality is that given in Eysenck, Arnold and Meili (1975), namely that:

> Personality is the relatively stable organisation of a person's motivational dispositions, arising from the interaction between biological drives and the social and physical environment. The term . . . usually refers chiefly to the affective-conative traits, sentiments, attitudes, complexes and unconscious mechanisms, interests and ideals, which determine man's characteristic or distinctive behaviour and thought.

This definition stresses not only the content of personality, but also that personality is *stable* (i.e. we do not change into different people from day to day), that it is *organised* (i.e. that its attributes are inter-related), that it is formed as a result of *interaction* between innate biological mechanisms and the environment, and that it is *distinctive* (i.e. that each personality is unique).

We shall adopt this as our basic definition, but we must make two further points. Firstly, the psychologist never uses 'personality' in the value-loaded sense often employed by the layman. Popularly, to have or to be full of 'personality' means to be outgoing, lively, and interesting, and to be lacking in it implies the opposite. But to the psychologist, everyone has personality. The emphasis is upon understanding people, not upon passing social judgements upon them. Secondly, the word 'character' is sometimes used synonymously with personality in ordinary conversation. The former comes from a Greek word meaning 'engraving', while the latter is from a Latin one meaning 'mask'. The former would thus seem to be something deep and fixed (i.e. innate), and the latter something superficial (i.e. acquired). Paradoxically, some psychologists take the former to mean acquired attributes and the latter to mean innate. This is confusing, and we shall in consequence avoid the term character, and stick to personality, taking it to refer to both innate and acquired factors.

1

Personality determinants

The teacher has an obvious interest in the determinants of personality. Only by knowing where personality comes from can he decide the extent to which the personalities of the children in his class are fixed by what happens outside school, and the extent to which they can be altered by what happens inside it. If we look back to the definition of personality that we quoted on page 3, we can see that we have already committed ourselves to the view that personality is the result of interaction between inherited and environmental factors, and we need now to look at the evidence for this view, taking heredity first.

THE INFLUENCE OF HEREDITY UPON PERSONALITY

Common observation has always led people to believe that we each inherit something of our personalities. We say that Mary has her father's calmness, that John has his mother's love of music, that Peter has his grandfather's determination. We describe people as born optimists or pessimists, as born teachers or nurses or comedians. But common observation could be wrong in ascribing these things to inheritance. They could just as easily be acquired through the close contacts which children have with their parents during the early formative years of their lives. Mary may have learnt the value of calmness from the calm way in which her father treated her, Peter may be determined because his mother admired this quality in her own father and sought to encourage it in her son, and the 'born' comedian may simply have found that making people laugh was the one sure way to get their attention when he was a boy.

The difficulty of separating the relative influence of heredity and environment in any area of psychological development is considerable (witness, for example, the continuing debate over the origins of measured intelligence). From the moment of birth onwards — indeed from the moment of conception, since the inter-uterine environment is itself important — heredity and environment interact with each other in a highly complex way. Many of the experiments which might help the psychologist to distinguish their relative importance, such as keeping the individual in a strictly controlled environment from birth, and denying him certain kinds of potentially valuable stimuli, are unacceptable for ethical reasons (which is one of the reasons why the psychologist so often falls back upon experiments with animals), and more often than we care to admit, the limited experiments that we can carry out produce conflicting results.

Some of our strongest evidence for the role of heredity in personality comes, therefore, not from psychology but from our knowledge of the biological mechanisms of inheritance. A good, simple account of these mechanisms is given in Mussen, Conger and Kagan (1974), and all that we need to say here is that at conception each normal child, with the exception of identical twins, receives his unique complement of forty-six chromosomes, twenty-three from each parent, and that these chromosomes contain the genes responsible for the transmission of attributes from the parents to the child. Our biological knowledge is not yet sufficiently advanced to tell us which precise genes transmit which precise attributes, but it is known that physical characteristics such as potential height and weight, colour of hair and eyes, size of feet and hands and so on, are all in some way genetically determined. Importantly for our purposes, there is also evidence that genes play a part in determining individual differences in behaviour.

Much of this evidence comes from studying people who have inherited chromosomal, and therefore genetic, abnormalities of one kind or another. For example, Down's syndrome (mongolism), which accounts for some fifteen per cent of patients in institutions for the subnormal, is present in individuals who have inherited an extra chromosome. Turner's syndrome, which produces abnormal shortness together with diminished mental ability, attention span, and memory, shows itself in girls who lack the normal complement of sex chromosomes. And choreoathetosis, a disease in which children exhibit spastic symptoms, self-mutilation, and extreme aggression, seems likely also to be due to an inherited defect. Finally, Price and Whatmore (1967) have produced evidence suggesting that among men who have inherited an extra male sex chromosome, there is a greater than normal incidence of instability and severe personality disorder, of early conviction for delinquent offences, and of eventual committal to institutions for the mentally subnormal and violent offender.

Of course, the fact that chromosomes are implicated in certain kinds of abnormal behaviour does not mean that they are necessarily also implicated in normal behaviour, but it does provide useful pointers in that direction. Following a similar clue, we can also look at those children who inherit identical chromosomes at conception, i.e. identical twins, and see if their personalities are any more alike than are those of fraternal twins. Identical, or monozygotic twins (M2 for short), are formed from a single ovum and a single sperm which, in the course of normal cell division, split completely into two separate embryos, while fraternal, or dizygotic (D2) twins, are formed from two separate ovums and two separate sperms and are no more alike genetically than are any other siblings.

Assuming that the twins in each M2 and D2 pair are brought up in similar environments, if M2 twins do prove to resemble each other more closely than do D2 we would be justified in seeing this as evidence for heredity. Research, in fact, shows the existence of just such a resemblance. Eysenck (1956) found closer similarities between M2 than D2 twins on two measures of personality which he calls neuroticism and extraversion (see chapter 5 below), while Stagner reports them to be more alike on occupational interests and free association responses. In a comparison between ordinary siblings as well as twins, Cattell and his colleagues (1955) concluded that heredity weighs more heavily than environment on such personality traits as warm-heartedness and sociability.

So far so good, but the problem has further complications. M2 twins and D2 twins may *not* enjoy similar environments. M2 twins, who are always of the same sex, and who resemble each other closely physically, are often treated consciously much more alike by their parents than are D2 twins. They are also treated more alike by other adults and by school friends, many of whom cannot tell them apart. The only way to avoid this problem is to look at instances where M2 and D2 twins have been separated at birth and each brought up in a different home. An early study by Newman, Freeman and Holzinger (1937) concluded that even here M2 twins resembled each other on personality measures more closely than did D2, while Shields (1962) found that on Eysenck's measures of extraversion and neuroticism, the resemblance between M2 twins was so much greater than that between D2 that even M2 twins reared apart were more alike than D2 reared together.

Fortunately from a humane point of view, but unfortunately from that of the researcher, instances of M2 twins reared apart are rare, and we cannot regard the samples in the above studies as large enough to put the matter beyond dispute. Taking the whole range of twin studies however, and applying statistical techniques, Eysenck has attempted to answer the question as to *how much* of the measurable personality differences between people is due to heredity and how much to environment, and has concluded that for his own measures of neuroticism and extraversion at least, the balance in favour of heredity may be as high as three to one (Eysenck and Eysenck 1969).

More evidence for the role of heredity comes from studies which seek a relationship between physique and personality. We know that the former is genetically strongly influenced, and if it can be established that certain kinds of physique usually go with certain kinds of personality, this might argue a genetic basis for the latter as well. If we go back to common observation again, we find that people have long claimed the physique-personality relationship to exist. The ancient Greeks, who studied man almost as keenly as the modern psychologist, held that people resembled in temperament those animals they most closely resembled in appearance (perhaps there are still echoes of this when we describe people as sheepish, or bovine, or wolfish, or owl-like) while Shakespeare's reference to men with a 'lean and hungry look' as being more thoughtful and dangerous than those who are fat has passed into popular speech, along with many other examples of his acute observations about his fellow men.

Whether the modern psychologist can improve very much upon the Greeks and Shakespeare in this field is open to question, but extensive work in it has been carried out over the last quarter-century and more by the American William Sheldon. On the basis of studies with male college students, Sheldon has postulated the existence of three basic types of body-build, the *endomorph*, who is round and fat, the *mesomorph*, who is hard and muscular, and the *ectomorph*, who is lean and delicate. Personality tests with the same sample revealed that each body build seems to have a corresponding set of personality characteristics:

> *the endomorph* is tolerant, complacent, sociable, easy-going, affectionate, and dependent
> *the mesomorph* is aggressive, tough-minded, competitive, energetic, and dominating
> *the ectomorph* is restrained, withdrawn, intellectual, and anxious.

Nobody belongs exclusively to only one of these types. We each of us have elements of all three in us, and in measuring a person's physique Sheldon assigns him a score from one to seven on each of them (known as his *somatotype*). Thus an extreme endomorph might score 7-1-1, an extreme mesomorph 1-7-1, and an extreme ectomorph 1-1-7. In practice, such extremes are rare, though in most people one of these scores will predominate over the other two.

Subsequent studies have shown a similar situation to exist for women, and for both women and men it has been asserted that the somatotype can be assessed reliably from age six onwards, and that it remains relatively constant throughout life (e.g. Sheldon 1954). True, many people put on weight or get more muscular as they grow older, but since endomorphs put on more weight than do people with other builds, and mesomorphs more muscle, the somatotype remains, in comparison with other people in the same age group, more or less the same.

Unfortunately, Sheldon's findings have not been fully confirmed by other investigators. Some claim not to have found the same three physical types, while others doubt the relationship between them and personality. However, more recent work by Sheldon (Sheldon et al. 1969) has uncovered further corroborative evidence, and his assertions seem, partially at least, to be well founded. It would be nice to leave it at that, and to move on to our next point, but once again we must admit to a snag. Sheldon's findings might have nothing to do with heredity at all. Muscular people may be more aggressive and competitive than fat or thin people simply because life has taught them that with their physical strength aggression and competitiveness pay off, while thin people, who find the reverse to be true, retire discreetly to their books. Alternatively, though less likely, child rearing practices may be responsible, with the fat person developing both his broad waistline and his love of comfort in response to an over indulgent mother.

Sheldon keeps an open mind on these matters, and the most reasonable conclusion is that both heredity and environment lie behind the physique-personality relationship. From an educational point of view, Sheldon's work is of added interest because correlations have been found to exist between the somatotype and, respectively, personality disorders and educational achievement. For example, samples of delinquent youths have been shown to contain a significantly large percentage of mesomorphs (Glueck and Glueck 1956), while samples of good honours degree holders have been found to show a significant tendency towards ectomorphy (Parnell 1958). Eysenck has suggested in the past that if the somatotype does give us an insight into inherited personality characteristics, it would be of use to take a simplified measurement of it, based upon height-weight ratio and chest girth, as a part of the routine school medical examination. This would give us a clue, from an early age, to the trend of a child's future personality development, and would help us to avoid making demands upon him which he is temperamentally unable to fulfill. However, it might have the corresponding disadvantage of serving as a self-fulfilling prophecy.

Another approach to the relationship between heredity and personality is the longitudinal study. We look for any evidence of temperamental differences between babies in the early days of life, when environment has had little chance to exert any influence, and then follow them through into later life to see if these differences are still apparent. One of the best longitudinal studies is that of the American researchers Thomas, Chess and Birch (1970). Taking a sample of 141 children, initially aged eight to twelve weeks, the researchers obtained ratings for them from parents and social workers on such items of behaviour as activity levels, regularity of bodily functions (feeding, sleeping, etc.), adaptability, sensitivity to stimuli, and disposition (cheerful, cranky, etc.). Results showed that sixty-five per cent of the children could be assigned unequivocally to one of three groups:

> *the easy group*, characterised by regular body functioning, adaptability, a positive approach to new people and objects, low reaction levels, and cheerfulness of mood (forty per cent of sample)
> *the difficult group*, characterised by irregular body functioning, low adaptability, a negative approach to new people and objects, over-reaction to stimuli, and negativity of mood (ten per cent of sample)
> *the slow to warm-up group*, characterised by low activity levels, low adaptability, some withdrawal in the face of new people and objects, mild reaction levels, and slight negativity of mood (fifteen per cent of sample).

The sample has now been followed through childhood and into adolescence, and membership of the groups has remained markedly constant. Not surprisingly, the *easy group* have presented fewer problems. When they started school, they proved readily adaptable, joined in activities, and learnt rules quickly. Only eighteen per cent of them have developed behaviour problems, as opposed to seventy per cent of the *difficult group*.

Obviously environmental factors will by now have played some part in heightening or diminishing these temperamental characteristics, but that environment is not the *cause* of them is evidenced by the fact that the researchers have found parental behaviour styles to be evenly distributed across the three groups of children. Where these styles have been an important variable, however, is in the success with which each group of children has come to terms with these characteristics. Easy children have flourished under most parental styles (this would probably not have been so had there been any really bad parents in the sample), but the difficult children have become increasingly awkward and negative if reared by inconsistent, impatient, or excessively punitive parents. Difficult children, it seems, need extra skilful, objective and painstaking handling. And the same appears to be true of those who are *slow to warm-up*. The last named children have shown a particular need for encouragement and parental support. Without it, or in the face of abrupt precipitation into new experiences, they have tended to withdraw even further into themselves. The key to success with them seems to have been to present them with plenty of new and interesting stimuli, but to allow them to tackle this stimuli at their own pace, providing plentiful praise and guidance, and encouraging them not to give up in the face of difficulties.

Thomas, Chess and Birch's findings that early temperamental characteristics provide a reliable guide to future personality development confirms the work of earlier researchers such as Escalona and Heider (1959). It puts us in a position (taken together with the other areas that we have mentioned in this chapter) to agree with Allport (1961) that what we seem to inherit is the raw material of our personality ('temperament' is as good a word for this raw material as any). Environment, in ways which we shall be examining in the next section, then moulds this raw material into its mature form. The importance of this to the teacher is emphasised by Thomas, Chess and Birch themselves. They point out that temperament affects a great deal of what a child does in school, from the way in which he relates to his teacher and other children, to the way in which he tackles the learning task. A child with high activity levels is likely to become frustrated and fidgety if made to sit still for too long, a child with a short attention span may respond well only in an environment with plenty of variety, a slow to warm-up child may need repeated and patient exposure to a learning task before he becomes confident enough to be able to tackle it, and a child with a negative and whimsical disposition may become worse if his own mood is matched with a similar one, or with anger and a battle of wills, by the teacher.

Of great relevance to the more general debate on teaching methods, Thomas, Chess and Birch found that an over-permissive atmosphere was particularly unsuitable for the difficult child, who did better on clear and patient guidance from the teacher in a more formal and structured classroom. It seems probable that the slow to warm-up child might well also flourish more in such a classroom, and might run the risk of passing unnoticed in a particularly open and active environment.

This doesn't mean that we are entering a plea for formal teaching methods. Far from it. But it does mean that there is no single set of methods which is of optimum benefit for all children. An active, outgoing, sociable child may do much better in an informal than in a formal setting, and the opposite may be true of a more withdrawn or hesitant child. So whatever methods the teacher uses, he must be alert to children as individuals, which is very difficult in a large class, but which is an essential aspect of the teacher's role. We shall be returning to this point at greater length in the next section.

ENVIRONMENT

Having established the importance of heredity in personality, we now turn to environment. The obvious place to start is in the home, where the child spends all his early years and a large proportion of his later ones. Within the home, most research interest has focused on the mother-child relationship. It is the mother who normally supplies the child with much of his stimuli. It is she who feeds him, cares for him, plays with him, and decides what behaviour is acceptable and unacceptable from him. It is she who provides him with love, and with an audience for much of his early activity. It is she who takes him to school when he grows older, and she to whom he tells his problems. This is not to minimise the role of the father, nor is it to ignore the fact that some of the mother's role is often shared with other adults. We shall have more to say about this later. It is simply to stress that for the majority of children, the mother provides the main human link with the outside world in the early years of life.

One way of seeing how important this link actually is in the formation of the child's personality is to look at those instances where the child has been deprived of it through maternal death or neglect. In a series of studies, Goldfarb (e.g. 1955) compared two groups of orphans, one of whom had been brought up in institutions for the first three years of their lives prior to fostering, and the other of whom had been placed in foster homes at a much earlier age. At adolescence, the children in the first group were found to be far less mature and emotionally stable than the second. Although making many demands upon their foster parents, they seemed incapable of relating warmly to them or to anyone else. They were relatively apathetic, and showed signs of linguistic and mental backwardness.

This study seems to show two things. Firstly that maternal deprivation in the first three years of life leaves a permanent mark upon the personality, and secondly, that as the group who had been placed early in foster homes seemed to be developing normally, a good foster mother is a satisfactory substitute for a natural mother. Other studies have produced similar findings.

To take just one example, Williams (1961) found that eighty per cent of a sample of children in care aged between five and eleven who could not relate satisfactorily to their foster parents had been deprived of mothers or of mother substitutes during the first two years of life.

What these studies don't tell us is which aspects of maternal care are the most important, or whether indeed these aspects differ from child to child dependent upon temperament. It is also fair to point out that some institutions offer a good level of substitute care, and that some children from even the worst kinds of institutions have turned out well. Our point of emphasis must be, I think, that with most children, the absence of the warm and supportive relationship which normally exists between the child and his mother (or mother substitute) makes it much more difficult for them to form satisfactory relationships as they grow older.

We shall be enlarging upon this point further in the next chapters, but before we leave this quick survey of research evidence into maternal deprivation we ought to see what happens when the child remains with his mother but is neglected by her. Robertson (1962) produces a number of case studies which dramatically illustrate the point. She found that children who were brought up with adequate physical care but by mothers who, through emotional problems of their own, seemed unable to respond to them with real warmth or affection, demonstrated 'less reaching out to the environment' (to use Robertson's own phrase) than did normal children. They tended to be docile, to cry less than usual, and to show less animation and less signs of real pleasure. At nursery school, they showed a lack of muscular tone, their 'flabby limpness' and 'clumsy unco-ordination' contrasting markedly with the 'strong sturdiness' and 'directed and skilful movements' of the children from good homes.

These findings fit in well with an earlier study by Sears, Macoby and Levin (1957), whose research showed that even amongst mothers who appeared well adjusted, a generally cold, strict and partially rejecting mothering style led to a higher level of feeding problems, of over-dependency, of poor socialisation, and of weak initiative amongst young children than did a warm and more permissive approach. They also fit in well with studies with animals, and in particular with the work of Harold Harlow at the University of Wisconsin. We shall refer to animal studies in this book only rarely, but Harlow's work seems to have such obvious relevance for human behaviour, that it cannot very well be left out.

What Harlow did was to raise several generations of rhesus monkeys under conditions of varying degrees of maternal deprivation, and study the results. In an early experiment, infant monkeys were taken away from their mothers at birth and kept isolated in individual cages equipped only with artificial *surrogate mothers*, simple wire models provided in some cases with feeding bottles and in others with a covering of a towelling material that provided the young monkey with soft tactile contact. Harlow found that this tactile contact seemed of great importance to the monkeys. Where a monkey was in a cage with both kinds of surrogate mother, he would have to feed at the wire one, but he would voluntarily spend most of his time with the towelling one, clinging to her soft surface with every sign of contentment and pleasure. When he was challenged by the introduction of a frightening stimulus into his cage, he would invariably run to the latter for comfort, viewing the stimulus with apparent curiosity from the safety of his perch.

These findings led Harlow to conclude that it is the actual tactile contact between a mother and her child that plays the major part in the growth of love between the two, and that allows the latter to develop satisfactorily. These findings seemed to be strengthened by the fact that monkeys who were raised with only a wire mother surrogate, and without the towelling one, showed every sign of emotional disturbance and withdrawal. They spent most of their time in the corner of their cages, rocking quietly to themselves, and cowered in terror when a frightening stimulus was brought near them. They fed at the wire mother surrogate, but spent little time with her otherwise. When taken outside their cages, they showed no confidence in exploring their environment, in marked contrast to the towelling reared monkeys, who as long as their surrogate mother was present to provide a refuge in case of threat, took great interest in the toys and the building blocks that had been placed there for their use. Harlow was even prompted to conclude that the towelling mothers were in some ways better than real ones, since they were always available, and never became impatient or scolded their young!

However, no doubt to the relief of mothers generally, Harlow was forced to revise this opinion when his infant monkeys grew older (Harlow and Harlow 1962). From the age of three to five years, monkeys raised with towelling mothers turned out to show many of the behaviour problems of those raised with wire ones. When allowed to mix with other monkeys, they were unable to relate to them satisfactorily either socially or sexually. Those females who eventually became mothers (entirely, it seems, through the patience and persistence of a group of normally reared males), proved themselves to be in Harlow's words 'hopeless, helpless and heartless' at the job, either ignoring their offspring or abusing them cruelly.

What Harlow's work seems to show is that although certain things like the provision of tactile contact are an important part of mothering, mothering itself is a very complex function, and unless the child receives an adequate amount of it (what represents an adequate amount may, of course, differ from child to child), then his chances of normal development, or indeed of becoming a satisfactory parent himself in adult life, are likely to be permanently blighted. Later experiments by Harlow (Harlow and Harlow 1966) lead him to suggest that the major damage is done if deprivation takes place for the first six months of the infant monkey's life, which is roughly equivalent to the first two or three years of human life. Deprivation for the first sixty days of a monkey's life — the first six months or so of human life — is in Harlow's opinion probably reversible in its effects, given adequate subsequent care and attention. By one year of age, Harlow concludes, the deprived human child may have sustained 'enduring emotional scars, and by two years (may have) reached the point of no return'.

Evidence for the importance of environment in personality development does not come only from the home. Numerous studies have shown that children brought up in a middle class culture tend to have measurable differences in personality from those brought up in a working class one. McCandless (1969) has it that middle class standards and values lead children to espouse hard work, ambition, cleanliness and self-control (particularly in relation to aggression and sex), while those of the working class result in children who are more open and uninhibited, and more inclined towards the immediate gratification of needs and impulses. The greater incidence of aggressive, violent and delinquent behaviour amongst working class children is argued to be directly attributable to the poorer training in social control and to the greater economic and social deprivation and frustration that these children experience (e.g. McDonald 1968). Sociological research shows that some working class sub-groups develop their own sub-cultures which espouse forms of behaviour that are at variance with what is taught at school and by the law of the land. Often these sub-groups lay positive emphasis upon toughness, quick wits, excitement and the desirability of resisting restraint, and whether he likes it or not, the child grows up believing that such things are the norm until he starts school and comes into conflict with a quite different order of things.

On a wider canvas still, anthropologists have shown us that identifiable personality differences exist between national or tribal groups. One of the most celebrated of all such investigations is that by Margaret Mead. Mead (1935) found that three primitive New Guinea tribes, although similar ethnically, differed markedly from each other in behaviour. The Arapesh were co-operative, gentle, unassertive and friendly, while the Mundugumor appeared violent, aggressive, competitive and suspicious. The third tribe, the Tchambuli, seemed to have reversed the sex roles, with the women doing the hunting and the trading (though not the fighting), while the men concentrated on artistic and non-utilitarian pursuits. Mead's findings are regarded nowadays as something of an over-simplification, but they are by no means out of keeping with more modern ones, such as those of Caudill and Weinstein (1966) on the personality differences between Japanese and American adolescents. It seems, then, that our social class and our national culture, as well as our more immediate environment within the family, can all influence the way in which our innate temperament develops.

From the point of view of the teacher, the particular importance of the findings quoted in this chapter on personality determinants is that the child who appears awkward or difficult, violent or aggressive, withdrawn or sullen, should not automatically be blamed for it. In our chapters on personality and learning theory, we shall be looking at how far psychologists hold us to be responsible for our own behaviour (and incidentally seeing that there is a fair measure of disagreement amongst them), but for the present we need to stress that a child's personality is not his own wilful creation. Teachers and others who are concerned with the alleged decline in standards of behaviour amongst the young are sometimes prone to blame it upon the influence that psychologists have had upon child-rearing practices. This is unfair. As we shall be saying throughout the book, the psychologist emphasises the importance of clear and consistent standards in the education of the young as much as, perhaps more than, the most ardent exponents of outmoded Victorian discipline. Where he differs from them is that he suggests that before we start trying to 'correct' a child, we first take the trouble to understand why he is as he is. Only then are the methods that we use to change him likely to be well chosen, and the changes beneficial to him as well as to us.

2

Personality development

The first three years of life, during which, as we have seen, the effects of maternal deprivation seem particularly hard to reverse, are an example of what the psychologist calls a *critical period* in the development of the child. A *critical period* is, in fact, any stage in human or animal development during which the organism is maximally sensitive to the presence of certain kinds of stimuli. Denied these stimuli, behaviour which is regarded as characteristic of the species concerned does not develop, even though there is often a considerable gap in time between the critical period and the age at which the behaviour normally occurs. Thus, deprived of mothering themselves in infancy, Harlow's monkeys grew up incapable of mothering their own young, and the same may well hold true for humans, as any veteran social worker who has watched the depressing cycle of aggressive and violent mothering styles pass from one generation to the next will readily attest.

One question that is sometimes asked is why should children who are shamefully treated by their mothers during this critical period often show great affection for them, even though they are incapable of showing it to anyone else? One answer is that proposed by Hess (1970), namely that in the early years of life children may have a natural tendency to seek proximity to other people, and that whoever happens to be proximate during the critical period becomes the object of an enduring attachment. The point Hess is making is that this attachment is a mechanical one. The child attaches himself to his mother simply because she happens to be there. There is no element of choice in the matter. Such an attachment would have obvious survival value, and may be akin to imprinting in animals, that instinct that prompts some creatures to attach themselves to the first moving object they see during the early hours of life, and to remain attached to it through thick and thin (however embarrassing this may prove to the object concerned, should it happen to be the research psychologist himself).

In an attempt to study the influence of the first three years of life upon subsequent development more closely, Bronson (1962) has conducted research which suggests that the extent of our involvement with other people may be particularly influenced by experiences in the first year of life, while our ability to behave independently and to cope with problems may be influenced by experiences in the third. Whether it is possible to be as precise as this with all children is by no means clear. It is probably safer to go in the opposite direction and to say that the whole of childhood is a critical period and that, so complex is human psychological development, there may be great variation between children as to which particular years of childhood are critical for which particular kinds of development. There may, as we indicated above, even be children who can survive severe maternal deprivation in the first three years or so of life, and yet still appear, on the surface at least, unscarred, but they are probably very few in number.

What we must stress is that what happens to the child during the critical period and sub-periods of childhood is not really analogous to the rational experiences of the adult, which happen to a physiologically mature organism and which can be viewed by him objectively and within the context of extensive previous experience. To the child, with his immature emotional and cognitive systems, the things that happen are assimilated at a much more fundamental level, and help define, for better or worse, the very meaning of being alive. A child brought up by a rejecting mother will see the world as a much more hostile place than will the child raised in happier circumstances. The child who always has to yell his head off to get attention will have a different idea of human relationships from the child whose wants are respected and satisfied. The child who is brought up in the shadow of his parents' unhappy marriage, or who constantly has demands made upon him that he is temperamentally unable to meet, will see the world as a more threatening place than will the child who enjoys more social harmony.

Though we need not dwell upon it, since there is no proof that it applies equally to humans, there is evidence that animals brought up in environmental impoverishment may even suffer physiological impairment. For example, Teyler (1975) reports evidence that rats raised in social isolation have a thinner cerebral cortex, less developed neural connections, and secrete less brain chemicals than do rats raised in a stimulating and enriched environment. Not surprisingly, the unfortunate creatures also perform less well on the kinds of discrimination problems that in humans are normally regarded as signs of intelligence. Such physiological impairment seems to be permanent. Because of their social isolation, the rats have been deprived of the possibility for physiological growth which is only open to them during the critical period concerned.

ERIKSON'S DEVELOPMENTAL STAGES
One approach to the subject of critical periods in human development is to see each of them as dominated by certain learning tasks which must be completed properly if the individual is to move satisfactorily on to the next period. One of the main proponents of this theory in the field of personality is Erik Erikson (b. 1902), until recently professor of human development in the University of Harvard. Erikson holds that in personality there are eight critical periods, or stages, spread out over the whole of the individual's life span, and he defines them in terms of the positive learning that takes place if they are successfully negotiated, and the negative learning that takes place if they are not (e.g. 1959). These eight stages are:

		Positive	Negative
1	early infancy	—	trust versus mistrust
2	late infancy	—	autonomy versus shame and doubt

3	early childhood	—	initiative versus guilt
4	middle childhood	—	competence versus inferiority
5	adolescence	—	identity versus role confusion
6	early adulthood	—	intimacy versus isolation
7	middle adulthood	—	generativity versus stagnation
8	late adulthood	—	self-acceptance versus despair

Erikson isolated these stages as a result of his experiences in clinical psychology both in Europe and America, and they are strongly influenced by psychoanalytical ideas which, as we shall see later in the book, admittedly not all psychologists are prepared to accept (chapter 3). However, Erikson does not propose that these stages represent all the critical learning tasks that the individual has to face if his personality is to develop successfully. All he suggests is that they are a useful way of looking at childhood and adulthood, and of isolating the point at which the child or the adult may go astray in his development. The eight stages are by no means hard and fast ones, and even though the individual may apparently come through each one satisfactorily, some negative learning will almost certainly take place, and may remain within the personality as a potential source of insecurity.

Erikson's ideas have proved very influential in the field of education, and his eight stages provide a convenient way for us to examine personality development. Let's take each one in turn, and discuss it within the context of the work of the teacher.

1 *Trust versus Mistrust*　Erikson accepts the critical importance of the child–mother (or mother substitute) relationship in the first three years of life. He divides these years into his first two developmental stages, *stage one* covering the first year, and *stage two* years two and three. In year one, Erikson sees all the various aspects of good mothering as combining to produce in the child a sense of trust. From his mother's love and care, from the attention which she devotes to his needs, from her ready provision of food and of tactile comfort, in short, from her

consistent presence as the satisfier of all his various needs, the child learns that the world around him is a place he can trust, a secure place in which he can safely consign his physical and emotional well-being to the good offices of others, in consequence becoming free enough to turn his attention to all the other interesting things that surround him.

Denied this sense of trust, the child is likely to become fearful and anxious, and, dependent upon temperament, either to have little energy or confidence for relating to the outside world, or to feel that he must take what he wants from it by aggression and hostility.

2 *Autonomy versus Shame and Doubt*   If he comes through this first stage successfully, the child's urge to reach out and explore the world is aided from the second year of life onwards by his growing physical competence. From the secure base of his trust in those around him, he sets out on a voyage of discovery. Inevitably, this voyage involves experimenting to find out the extent of his powers over the people and objects in his world, and just as inevitably, this involves him in the increasing exercise of his own will. Many psychologists (e.g. Valentine 1956) testify to the child's going through a particularly negative phase during the third year of his life, in which he appears deliberately to defy those around him. If thwarted, he may show temper tantrums and be aggressive and destructive. This seems to be a necessary part of his experimentation, and a necessary sign that he is beginning to see himself as a distinct, autonomous person, differentiated from those around him. The long term consequences of adult reaction to the child during this phase may well be considerable. If the adult meets him head on in a conflict of wills, then, dependent upon temperament, the child may become increasingly difficult, determined to make his own will prevail even at the cost of the feelings of conflict that this arouses in him, or he may abandon his attempt at asserting his autonomy, and become inhibited and full of doubts about himself.

Often it is difficult for adults to avoid this conflict of wills.

The child seems to be threatening adult authority, and that's not an easy thing to take from a two-year-old. But Valentine also reports evidence which seems to show that children who, probably for temperamental reasons, do not go through this negativistic phrase are frequently rated by their parents when they get to adolescence as lacking in initiative and spirit, and too easily led by others. The role of the adult should, therefore, be one of patience and understanding, a role in which the child's autonomy is respected and encouraged where practicable, and limited consistently and with gentle firmness where it is not. Thus the child will learn that the world is a place in which certain laws and standards obtain, within the limits of which he can do things for himself and take decisions for himself. By learning that control is not something that is always exerted upon him from outside, he will also begin to learn that he has responsibilities for self-control. Just as he can influence the behaviour of people and things in the world around him, so he can influence his own behaviour, and gain in consequence the rewards of adult approval which such self-control brings.

Erikson himself (1950) sums up the stage of *autonomy* versus *shame and doubt* by saying that it is decisive for the ratio within the child's future behaviour of 'co-operation and wilfulness, self-expression and its suppression. From a sense of self-control comes a lasting sense of good will and pride; from a sense of loss of self-control and of foreign overcontrol comes a lasting propensity for doubt and shame.'

3 *Initiative versus Guilt* This stage, which begins at the age of about three or four, is the first one in which the teacher is directly concerned. If the child has successfully consolidated his autonomy, he is now free to find out the extent to which he is allowed to put this autonomy to good effect. Increasing physical agility on the one hand, and increasing linguistic skills on the other, allow him to communicate more fully with the people and things around him, and to give more scope to his powers of initiative. In his expanding world, which now embraces the nursery school or the play-group as well as the home, he

discovers the extent to which he can exercise this initiative, and the extent to which it is to be restricted by others.

Since this period of development also marks the growth of moral behaviour and of the conscience, such restrictions, dependent upon the language in which adults express them, may lead to the child's feeling worthless and guilty for being as he is, and for wanting to do the things that he wants to do. He is also likely to be increasingly influenced by the behaviour of those around him, in particular of those older than him. His most important models of behaviour (*role models*) are usually his parents, and from this age onwards, the father often becomes an increasingly important influence in the child's life. Up to now, the father may have acted as a very efficient mother substitute, but from now on he begins to take up a more distinct role, as a provider of different kinds of experiences from those of the mother, and as the source of overall authority in the home.

From both parents, but particularly from the parent of the same sex, the child begins at this time to learn his definitive sex role. Some part of this sex role is, of course, biologically determined. Smith (1974) reviews evidence to show that in other primates besides man the male is more prone to engage in aggressive and in boisterous physical activity from infancy onwards than is the female, and that this difference disappears if the female's mother has been injected with male hormones during the pregnancy. But a significant part of it is learnt from parents, teachers, and the adult world in general. Violent activity is more readily countenanced in boys in our society than it is in girls. Certain pastimes are regarded as boyish, certain others as girlish. Books, toys, games, even colours are usually chosen for a child with his or her sex in mind.

What this means is that boys and girls have different kinds of limits placed upon their initiative. A boy who engages in girlish pursuits is made to feel uncomfortable and guilty about it, as is the girl who engages in boyish ones. Perhaps because of their traditional role in the home, girls have their initiative further curbed in that they are encouraged to be more dependent than boys. Lewis (1972) shows that this dependency training in girls is often evident from the second year of life onwards, and appears to continue right through into adolescence, and Davie and his colleagues (1972) show that girls are more anxious for parental approval than boys, while boys are more concerned with the approval of other children. Older siblings also help the child to learn his sex role. Koch (1956) has shown that boys with older sisters take more interest in girlish activities than do boys with only older brothers, while girls with older brothers show a corresponding interest in boyish things.

The growth of initiative has obvious implications for the kind of education that we ought to be offering to children at this stage in their lives. Assuming that we want to encourage this initiative, assuming that we want children to develop their sense of independence, assuming that we want them to grow in responsibility, and to be capable of taking decisions and of using their imagination, then the school or play group must give them opportunities to do these things. This means, of course, having the right kinds of equipment, the water and sand, the crayons, paints and clay, the building blocks and the constructional toys, the climbing frame, the home corner, the cooker, the dressing up clothes, the books, the musical instruments and the animals. But more than any of these, it means having the right kind of relationship with children. Teachers of the very young are dedicated people, and it would be quite wrong to talk of such a thing as 'teacher neglect' analogous to parental neglect, but there is a danger that in their relationship with children teachers may unwittingly be inclined to exercise the wrong sort of control over them.

We might enlarge on this. We wrote earlier that, dependent upon the language which adults use to enforce them, the restrictions that are laid upon a child may make him feel worthless and guilty for being as he is. Obviously, there are many things that children must be prevented from doing. What is important, though, is that the child should not be made to feel at odds with himself for wanting to do them. We shall be returning to this point of guilt and self-rejection in children when we come to discuss personality theories, particularly those of Carl Rogers in chapter 4. But it cannot be stressed too strongly that it is very damaging for a child to be made to feel that he is wicked or bad for wanting to behave as he does. These wants may stem from deep biological drives over which the child has no control. Labels like 'good' or 'bad' are quite inappropriate for these drives, and belong only to the way in which the child learns to control them and to channel them into socially acceptable forms.

This means that the teacher should always focus attention upon a child's action, rather than pass moral judgement upon the child himself. It is the action that is unacceptable, not the child. 'That wasn't a very kind thing to do', rather than 'you are an unkind boy'. 'That was a thoughtless thing to say' rather than 'you are an ungrateful girl'. The child's self-concepts, as we shall see later, are immature, fragile things. He gains his idea of the kind of person he is from listening to what the adults in his life tell him about himself. If they are constantly censuring him, and thus assuring him of his lack of worth, he may incorporate this negative picture into his own self-image, and not only feel guilt in consequence, but often come to produce the very sort of anti-social behaviour that he feels adults expect of him.

The teacher, like the parents, also acts as a role model for the child. The warmer the relationship between teacher and child, the more effective a model will she be. Any discipline which relies upon harshness, or upon the constant deprival of privileges, is likely to alienate the child, and dependent upon his temperament and home background, to frighten him, to antagonise him, or simply to make him withdraw his attention elsewhere. In all these cases, the teacher's function as an agent in the child's socialisation will be greatly diminished. The most satisfactory deterrent that the teacher has for unwanted behaviour is to withdraw her approval of it in the manner mentioned above, preferably at the same time suggesting an alternative, more acceptable activity.

As far as the child's developing sex role is concerned, it is important that all school activities are open to both sexes, and that different standards of behaviour are not demanded of them.

However, the teacher's influence in this sphere is not all embracing. The child will quickly learn his sex role outside school, and it would be wrong for the teacher to impose a form of unisexualism upon children that will expose them to ridicule in the home! The best that the teacher can hope for is that the child will grow up respecting the opposite sex.

4 *Competence versus Inferiority* Having learnt initiative, which frees the child to *do* things, he now faces the task of learning competence, which frees him to do them *well*. This stage, which lasts approximately throughout the primary school years, is marked by the child's growing physical and linguistic skills. In a few short years he moves from the world of infancy to something approaching an adult's physical co-ordination and verbal fluency. As he does so, he vastly increases his capacity for experience. As Piaget has shown us, he also develops new cognitive skills, in a relatively fixed order of progression, and uses them to comprehend and manipulate this experience.

These maturing skills profoundly influence the picture he builds of his environment. He asks questions, he interprets the answers, he watches how things behave, he tackles problems. And as every teacher knows, he goes about all these things in his own unique way. Further, not only is there a wide variation between different children, the same child has a pretty broad repertoire of responses himself. However well the teacher may know his class, he will be hard put to it to predict how individual children will react to many of the stimuli of everyday classroom life. At times, it seems as if the child is trying out different kinds of responses to the same stimulus simply to see which one works best, and often this is precisely what he is doing, experimenting, in fact, to see how the world behaves and to determine the extent to which his own skills allow him to influence this behaviour.

Sadly, as every teacher also knows, many children by this time are already showing signs of slipping inexorably behind the others in this business of acquiring skills. Sometimes they seem innately less able to ask the right kind of questions, and to comprehend the answers when they come. Others seem to have

missed the kinds of stimulation that we have been talking about
in the last chapter and in this. Failing to gain trust, autonomy,
or initiative — or sometimes all three — the child is
handicapped in his attempts to make use of his innate potential.
The older he becomes, the worse things often get. His failure to
master early skills renders him less able to master later ones.
Failure, like success, breeds upon itself. With each experience
of failure, he becomes less and less sure of himself, less and less
ready to tackle new things, less and less confident of his own
abilities. Conversely, the child who is developing competence
has the constant reassurance that his skills are an effective way of
dealing with the world, and of keeping a balance between its
demands and his own needs. With this competence comes the
increasing conviction of the world's consistency and predictabil-
ity, and of his own status and prestige within it. He develops a
defined personality, within an environment which he com-
prehends. And as he watches and identifies with his teachers and
his parents, so he can see that his own skills are a successful
version of the way in which they themselves go about the
business of living.

During the primary school years, the child discovers other
role models besides his parents and teachers of course. And this
discovery highlights more sharply than ever his developing
competence, or the lack of it. Principally, he discovers these
models amongst other children, and becomes increasingly
aware of their levels of competence in relation to his own. Other
children do things better or worse than he does, other children
get better or worse marks, get more or less praise from the
teacher, are more or less popular with the rest of the class, get
into trouble more or less often. And whether we like it or not, as
teachers we help this process of comparison along. We draw
attention to good work, we withold approval from bad, we
assign classroom jobs, we give extra help. The very uniqueness
of children makes it impossible to treat them all alike.

In the last section, we described the effect that the teacher
can have upon the child's feelings of guilt and self-rejection.
Unfortunately, little research has been carried out on the

influence that teachers have on the child's concepts of competence and mastery. But significant evidence of the role which parents play in this area comes from the work of Stanley Coopersmith in the USA. Coopersmith (e.g. 1968) has followed a group of boys through from age ten to early adult life, and has found that on the basis of psychological tests and of self and teacher ratings they have divided consistently throughout into three groups which he has labelled *high, medium* and *low* self-esteem. *High* self-esteem boys were from the beginning active and expressive; they enjoyed joining in, and were generally successful academically and socially. They were confident, not unduly worried by criticism, and had an accurate picture of their own abilities. *Medium* self-esteem boys shared many of these qualities, but were more conformist, more anxious for social acceptance, and less sure of their own worth. The *low* self-esteem boys were, by contrast, what Coopersmith calls a sad little group, isolated, fearful, self-conscious, reluctant to participate, and very sensitive to criticism. They were prone to underrate themselves, and were pre-occupied with their own problems.

What was of particular interest was that membership of these three groups did not appear to be particularly correlated with physical attractiveness, intelligence, or affluence (all came from middle class homes). But in examining their backgrounds Coopersmith found that the high self-esteem boys came from homes in which they were regarded as significant and interesting people, and in which their views on family decisions were invited and listened to. Parental expectations were more consistent and were higher than in the other two groups, and discipline was less permissive, though it depended more upon rewards than upon withdrawal of love or upon corporal punishment. The boys praised their parents' fairness. The low self-esteem boys, on the other hand, often rated their parents as unfair. There was little sign that their parents were interested in them or gave them clear guidance, and standards of discipline were inconsistent, veering unpredictably from extreme permissiveness to extreme strictness.

These findings are of interest to teachers not only for the light which they throw on children's backgrounds, but because they can be applied equally well to the classroom. The high self-esteem boys were generally successful in what they did, set themselves high goals, and worked more nearly to their potential, because they were not inhibited by the fear of failure, or by uncertainties as to their worth. If one has a realistic knowledge of, and confidence in, one's own skills, one is less wounded by the occasional failure, less deflated by the odd criticism, less anxious for the unqualified approval of all and sundry. One is readier to participate, less overawed by things, less daunted by possible pressures. The high self-esteem boys knew they counted as people because their parents, directly and indirectly, told them so. By the same token, the teacher can show his children that they count. He can encourage them to use their abilities, urge them on when they fail instead of punishing this failure by word or deed, take a close interest in their day to day progress, share their pleasure in success. It is one of the golden rules of the remedial teacher that the classroom must be so structured that each child can experience this success, no matter how low his personal level of ability happens to be, and the same rule should apply with equal strength in the normal classroom.

Interestingly, the high self-esteem boys had parents who set standards, and applied them consistently, and who were not unduly permissive. We have already mentioned the importance of consistency when dealing with children, and this is perhaps the point at which we should give it particular stress. It is through his experience of consistency in others that the child gradually learns that the world is a predictable place, and that the skills he acquires today will be of some value tomorrow as well. The infant's sense of trust, the older child's sense of self-esteem, are all based upon the security of knowing that the things in the world around us have patterns and laws. Water isn't dry today and wet tomorrow. People aren't kind to you one minute and cruel the next. The presence of standards in the classroom, standards that are related to the individual child's potential, gives the child a pattern against which to measure his own progress, something to aim for, proof of his own growing competence.

By setting standards, the teacher emphasises even further to children his interest in them. In all walks of life, if we are interested in anything, whether it be gardening or the local football team, we usually show this interest by a concern for standards of performance. Our garden, or mine at least, will never be like Kew, and our football team may never win the European Cup, but nevertheless, within the limits of what are possible, we have standards for them. An absence of any standards is often an indication that the thing, or the person, concerned, is really not worth bothering about. In the classroom, the presence of standards shows the child that we believe in him and want to see him make progress, and shows him also that the thing we are asking him to do, the skill we are asking him to master, the knowledge we are asking him to acquire, is worth something as well.

None of this implies an absence of classroom democracy. It is significant that the high self-esteem boys came from homes in which they were encouraged to express their views, were consulted over family decisions, and were generally made to feel that they were important people. The boys praised, remember, their parents' fairness. Nor does it imply a harsh discipline. Parents relied upon encouragement rather than upon corporal punishment or the withdrawal of love. The withdrawal of love, or in the teacher's case the withdrawal of concern and of interest, are never likely to produce self-esteem in a child. He needs to feel that he matters enough to be always given these things, and that they are no more subject to change or withdrawal than are the natural laws that make the world a reliable place in which to live.

At the risk of extending this section too far, there are three other factors that have bearing upon the development of competence in a child. The first is sex. We have already looked at some of the differences in personality between boys and girls, and there is ample evidence to show that these differences are reflected in academic achievement. One of the most exhaustive longitudinal studies ever carried out, that of Davie and his colleagues (1972), shows that girls tend to talk earlier than boys, and to remain more verbally fluent than boys even after starting school. Perhaps because of this fluency, they are generally more successful than boys in learning to read. Even though the gap between the sexes has narrowed by the age of nine, there are known to be more backward readers amongst boys than amongst girls at all stages of compulsory schooling. Girls are also less likely than boys to suffer speech defects, are less likely to be accident prone (at least outside the home), and are less likely to be referred for special help to the child guidance clinic. Boys on the other hand are generally better at number work than are girls, and they tend to take a wider interest in events outside the home, and in how things are made and in how they work.

The precise reasons for these differences between the sexes are not known. Girls may, for cultural reasons, spend more time in the home and in conversation with their mothers than do boys, and they may spend more time in reading because they have fewer outlets in organised sport. We have seen from the reference to Davie's work in the last section that they are more anxious to please their parents, and this again may mean that they spend more time with them, and more time doing the things of which parents approve, such as school learning. But there are probably genetic reasons as well. In many areas, girls seem to mature physically more rapidly than boys, and this may mean that they are able to tackle certain skills at an earlier age than are boys.

The second factor that still needs to be mentioned is social class. One gap in the work of Coopersmith is that his sample consisted only of boys from middle class homes. It tells us nothing about self-esteem in working class children. However, evidence from elsewhere (e.g. Rosenberg 1965) tells us that working class children, especially working class boys, are lower generally in self-esteem than are those from the middle class. And if we return to Davie's work again, we find that both working class girls and boys show more of the personality characteristics normally associated with low self-esteem, such as aggression, withdrawal, depression, and hostility to adults, than do middle class children. Davie also shows that for all the areas of competence in school which he tested (oral skills, creativity, reading and number), working class children trail significantly behind their more socially favoured peers. The inescapable conclusion is that working class children are handicapped in their search for competence, doubtless by the higher level of maternal and paternal deprivation, the poorer amenities and facilities, the less clearly defined standards and values, that go with membership of their class.

We have to be careful here of course. It would be quite wrong to suggest that *all* working class children have poor backgrounds, or that *all* middle class children come from stimulating and loving homes. Many working class homes are excellent, and many middle class homes are barren alike of material and of emotional support. Coopersmith, remember, found many low self-esteem boys in middle class homes. It would also be wrong to suggest that middle class values are in all cases *better* than working class ones. All we are saying is that the incidence of deprivation is statistically higher in working class homes than in middle class ones, and that middle class values are closer to most of those that lead to success in school and in society generally. It is up to the reader to decide for himself whether this is a good or a bad thing.

The third factor to which we must make brief reference is family size. Back in the 1930s, the psychoanalyst Alfred Adler put forward the theory that family size and one's birth order within the family have a significant influence upon personality. Adler's theory was a somewhat elaborate and fanciful one, but some part of it at least seems to be supported by modern research. Several studies, most recently Davie, show an inverse relationship between family size and both school attainment and personality adjustment. Since this relationship holds good irrespective of social class, it rather looks as if the unavoidably reduced amount of parental attention, guidance, and verbal communication which the individual often receives in a large family has a deleterious effect upon a wide range of his behaviour. This effect becomes increasingly noticeable as family size increases beyond two children. Davie also noticed that in these families it seems to be the oldest child's school attainment and social adjustment that are the most heavily penalised, presumably because, being the oldest, he or she is left to fend for themselves by the parents more than are any of the others.

Before we leave the question of competence and personality development, perhaps we could take up just one point that we mentioned a few paragraphs ago. We said that, amongst other things, a high level of *hostility to adults* is a characteristic of some children, particularly working class children, who are low on self-esteem. This might seem strange, but the reason for it is not hard to seek. If a child finds that in everything he does in the school and at home he is reminded of the fact that he is just not as good as most other children of his age, he can either accept this knowledge and become one of the sad little children to whom Coopersmith refers, or he can try to protect what is left of his self-esteem by fighting back. If he is no good at the things he is asked to do at school, he can either accept that this means *he* is no good, or he can reject the things themselves, and announce to the world, with hostility or with bravado, that *they* are not worth doing. If he fails to measure up to the standards of the school, he is in effect saying, it is not I who am incompetent, it is the standards that are wrong.

5 *Identity versus Role Confusion*   Erikson sees all the stages through which the personality passes in its development as really stages in self-discovery. By finding out about his place in the world, by listening to what other people have to say about him, by identifying with adults and with other children, by comparing himself with his peers, the child gradually builds up a picture of the person he is. He forms an *identity*. This process comes to a head in adolescence, and by the end of adolescence Erikson sees the personality as basically formed. In the developmental stages which remain in adult life, the individual

is faced with coming to terms with, and making best use of, the kind of person he has become. The more successfully he weathers the crisis of adolescence, the more sure and realistic will this 'person' be, the clearer and better defined its identity. Should the individual fail in the self-discovery tasks that face him in adolescence, he will suffer from what Erikson calls *role confusion.* He will have no clear idea of the person he is, a prey to the many diverse and conflicting pressures of adult life, clinging for security to a rigid and artificial picture of himself that leaves no room for change.

The most important biological feature of adolescence is the arrival of physical and sexual maturity. This abrupt transition from childhood to adulthood causes all kinds of problems. It takes girls approximately four years, from the onset of the adolescent growth spurt at about twelve and a half, to reach adult stature, with boys starting and finishing about eighteen months later. The adolescent has learned to cope with the business of being a child, now he finds himself called upon to cope with the business of being an adult, and to cope with it in a complex industrial society which, partly because of the lateness of the school leaving age, is reluctant to accord him adult status. More primitive societies than ours, where the child is automatically granted the rights and responsibilities of adulthood at puberty, experience far fewer problems with this age group than we do. Sociologists have suggested that these problems are therefore more a product of our 'artificial' culture than of the biological changes of adolescence itself.

Be that as it may, there is no denying that these problems exist. Obviously, they vary in intensity from individual to individual, but most adolescents find that many of the concepts which they have built up during childhood seem suddenly outdated. What they now have to learn is whether the naughty boy necessarily becomes the bad man, whether the good boy necessarily becomes the good one. Naughtiness, which once may have seemed a downright nuisance to one's peers, may now come to be regarded by them as an admirable rejection of authority, while goodness may come to be seen as a furtive attempt to gain adult favours. To make matters worse, partly because of changes in hormonal balance, many adolescents are prone to wildly fluctuating moods. Love and affection towards those around them may suddenly change to irritation and even active dislike. Not surprisingly, this causes the adolescent great perplexity (to say nothing of what it causes to the adults in his life!). Who, hidden within this confusion, is the real person?

To complicate things still further, the adolescent often finds himself taking on the colour of his surroundings. He behaves one way with his friends, another way with his parents, another way with his teachers. Each of these ways seems to involve a quite different set of values, and to impose quite different demands upon him. If he belongs to a minority group, such as an immigrant community or a minority social group, these conflicting demands may be even worse. And whoever he is, he often seems to be faced with having to make important decisions without clear guidance, because there appears to be no experienced person who really understands his position.

Intellectually, the majority of adolescents achieve what Piaget calls the stage of formal operations, a major landmark in cognitive development. As a result, they are now capable of abstract and deductive reasoning, and it is this, together with his frustration at the adult world, that makes the adolescent so prone to question things. Abstract concepts like freedom, justice and equality now begin to mean something to him, and before the realities of adult life catch up with him, he often goes through a phase of intense idealism during which he wants to set the world to rights. It is partly this that often makes him espouse political and social causes, but there is another reason too, namely that in spite of his outward assurance, the adolescent is far from certain that his opinions, particularly when they are at variance with his teachers or parents, are really correct. The doubts that he has over his own identity stretch to these as well. He is still experimenting with himself, still trying out his adult clothes so to speak, and by supporting causes and joining things he experiences a sense of kinship that gives him confidence. If other people are rebelling against authority, and are prepared to let him become one of them, then his personal battles against teachers and parents must be justified too, or so he reasons.

The adolescent's partial rejection of the authority of his parents and teachers also makes him less inclined than hitherto to see them as role models. He finds alternatives, sometimes in cult heroes like sportsmen and pop stars, sometimes in his peer group. Indeed, the peer group becomes increasingly important to him, especially in matters of dress, speech and behaviour. Acceptance by the peer group is of great moment to him. He finds himself excessively concerned to conform to its norms, excessively on show to it in all he does. He may be acutely embarrassed by anything, such as late physical development, which sets him apart from these norms. The sex drive, which in males reaches its peak at about sixteen to eighteen years of age, also makes the adolescent take an increasing interest in the opposite sex, and to be unsuccessful in relationships with it may be a profound blow to both boys and girls, and may lead to negative self-concepts that will crucially affect decisions later in life about such things as vocation, friends, life style and marriage partner.

Adolescence is also a peak age for delinquent activity. Although delinquency, as we have already suggested, is a multi-causal phenomenon, whose origins stretch back into faulty adjustment early in childhood, the majority of delinquent acts tend to occur in children who are in or near the final year of compulsory schooling, precisely the time when they are most irked by their continuing lack of adult status. Their lower levels of aggression, their greater dependency, their more effective socialisation, and their earlier reconciliation to their role in life make girls less prone to delinquent activity than are boys, though over the last ten years delinquent acts in girls, particularly those involving violence, have been increasing proportionately faster than in boys (in America the ratio of one such act in girls to every five in boys is now reported to be down to one to three). This is probably a reflection of the changing status of women in our society.

Evidence from both Britain and America suggests that the

personality of the delinquent adolescent is characterised by hostility, suspicion, impulsiveness, and low self-control. Usually there are poor self-concepts, feelings of inadequacy and rejection, and of confusion and conflict (e.g. Conger and Miller 1966). In addition to maternal deprivation, parental styles in delinquent homes usually show those features noticed by Coopersmith in the background of low self-esteem boys, i.e. they are erratic, unpredictable, and contain little evidence of any genuine interest in children. Frequently the father is rejected as a role model by the son because of the former's weakness, drunkenness, or harshness (Andry 1960). The incidence of delinquency increases sharply as we move down the social classes, and typically the delinquent comes from a deprived urban area in which, as we saw in chapter 1, the community approves such values as toughness and a rejection of authority.

In delinquency there is probably also a temperamental factor at work. We mentioned in chapter 1 that Glueck and Glueck have found a high proportion of mesomorphs amongst delinquents, and it may be that the high leadership and aggressive qualities that mesomorphs have, when denied socially acceptable outlets, turn to the gang sub-culture which features so prominently in delinquent activity. Further evidence for a temperamental factor comes from the work of Eysenck, who finds that delinquent samples are significantly extraverted, which again suggests a high level of aggression and an innate need for external stimuli and excitement (see chapter 5).

Enough of the negative side of adolescence. It is not difficult to make adolescence seem a very unattractive stage in human development. In fact many teachers much prefer working with this age group to any other, and welcome the adolescent's potential for idealism and involvement. They also find it exciting to watch the personality develop in such a brief span from a childish to an adult one, and find great reward from the help that they can give to the process. Part of their secret in dealing successfully with adolescents is that they seem aware of the experimental nature of much of what the adolescent does.

By their tolerance, but at the same time by the clear and consistent standards which they maintain in areas where such standards are not negotiable, they help the adolescent to answer the questions which he is posing of his environment, and to understand the limits that exist in the new grown-up world that he is about to enter.

They also seem aware of the depths of feeling and the vulnerability that underlie the sometimes brash and cynical adolescent exterior. Faced with the problem of achieving an identity in which the various parts of his personality enter into a consistent relationship with each other and are not lost in role confusion, the adolescent feels profound self-doubts, and needs the security of knowing that his teacher has confidence in the kind of person that he is becoming. The brashness and the cynicism are often no more than a defensive screen, erected to hide inner sensitivities and to impress the peer group. The teacher sees through the screen, though he is careful not to puncture it, particularly in front of the rest of the class, because this kind of humiliation can only lead to shame and loss of face for the adolescent, and often to a subsequent unforgiving hostility towards the teacher.

Teachers who understand adolescents also seem aware of the continuing need to show an interest — though never an intrusive one — in the adolescent's activities. This means his activities outside school as well as inside, and in his future prospects and ambitions as well as in his present performance. Such teachers also show an interest in his likes and dislikes. They listen to and respect his opinions, they tolerate his desire to be different from his elders, and they don't make glib judgements about his personality from such externals as fashions in appearance, speech, or dress. They encourage him to bring into the classroom as a fit subject for discussion his problems over personal and sexual relationships, and they are prepared to give clear answers to his questions, and to indicate the difference in the field of values between fact and belief, both of which have their place but which involve different kinds of issues.

They also understand the conflict, now often brought into sharper focus than ever in some children's lives, between the standards of school and those of the home. Any direct conflict between home and school can greatly increase the pressures towards role confusion in the child. Often the school can best reconcile these pressures by avoiding the unnecessary rules and restrictions which give the child the impression that school is out of touch with the real world. In any community, rules are necessary if people are to live together in harmony, but these rules should exist clearly and obviously for that end, and not to serve outmoded customs, or the prejudices of one small group. The more democratic the process that can be used to arrive at rules, the more point everyone sees in them, and the more likely they are to be obeyed. Bad rules, which are inevitably ignored as soon as those responsible for them have their backs turned, lead only to a loss of respect for authority, and a consequent flouting of many other rules that are there for a much better purpose.

There is some evidence that by a policy of rejecting the least able children in its own midst, a school can also cause its own kinds of conflicts and sub-cultures. Hargreaves (1967) and Lacey (1970) discovered (independently of each other) that secondary modern and grammar schools were instrumental in creating similar 'A' and 'C' stream mentalities, the former characterised by acceptance of the school, of its staff, and of its values, and the latter by their rejection. This is not the place to enter the debate about streaming, which has implications beyond those associated with personality, but the point is that where schools feel the need to separate children by ability, this should be done in a way which protects the self-esteem of the less able as well as of the more able.

Finally, teachers who work well with adolescents seem to understand that it is no good looking for the obedience and dependency in them which they had when younger. It is a failure to show this understanding that leads to many of the conflicts which parents have with adolescent sons and daught-ers. Refusal to accept that the adolescent is growing up only makes him assert his right to independence all the more strongly. Teachers who recognise this right take care to give him every reasonable opportunity to demonstrate his growing ability to take adult responsibility. Such opportunities are of far more value than any number of homilies directed at him by the adults in his life on the *need* for him to develop this responsibility. Too often when we lecture adolescents, and indeed younger children, on the desirability of their acquiring a maturer approach to life, we mean that they should acquire it only when it suits us, and at other times revert to the subordination of an earlier stage in their development. This is a misguided practice, and perhaps if we all realised it we would have less reason in education to bemoan the 'irresponsibility' of the young.

6 *Intimacy versus Isolation*   This stage, which occurs in early adulthood, is more the direct concern of teachers involved in higher and further education, but it is of relevance to all teachers in that it is the culmination of the years of childhood and adolescence. Intimacy is the ability to have full and satisfying personal relationships with other people of both sexes, relationships which culminate in marriage, in life-long friendships, and in close and sustaining contacts with the people with whom one works, and with the people in one's community.

Perhaps the best way of discussing this stage is to merge it with the wider discussion of the mature personality, that is with a discussion of those personal qualities that mark people out as having attained a balance and a richness in their development that allows them to live full and satisfying lives. Erikson has himself written widely on the mature personality, but the psychologist who has centred most attention on it is probably Gordon Allport (1897-1967). Allport (1961) sees the acquisition of a real sense of personal identity in adolescence as meaning that the individual has developed from being essentially a number of different people to being a single, or whole person. In the early stages of our personality development, Allport sees us as possessing a wide range of *traits*, such as friendliness, honesty, bookishness, which we use somewhat inconsistently and arbitrarily in our dealings with other people (e.g. we are honest with our friends but not with our teachers, bookish at school but not at home). As we grow older, many of these coalesce into a smaller number of better integrated units which Allport calls *selves* (e.g. we have one recognisable self for school, another for home), and, with the discovery of identity, these come together in turn to form the single unit of the mature personality.

To Allport, the mature personality is, therefore, characterised by co-ordination and consistency. If a person is mature, we know that whatever the situation in which we meet him he remains identifiably the same person (within reasonable limits at least; every personality may break down under extreme stress). He is not honest at home and dishonest at work (or honest and dishonest at both home and work in different circumstances), or pious at church and amoral at the local club, or humorous with his friends and a wet blanket with his family, or confident with men but a pitiful stammerer with women. He does not, in fact, still have several different selves, each one of them capable of its own separate codes of behaviour and of values. An extreme example of people who had failed to achieve this mature integration were the nazi concentration camp officers who were reputedly good husbands and fathers in the evenings, but spent their days sending innocent people to a hideous death.

Of course, this is not all there is to maturity. Usually when we talk of the mature personality we imply a value judgement in that we expect his integrated personality to have qualities that make him desirable to the community as a whole. It is possible, in theory at least, for a person to be entirely integrated in doing evil, which might mean that he meets Allport's criterion, but is hardly the sort of person we would want to have as a neighbour or as a teacher of children. We also usually think of the mature person as being an effective person, as being good at getting things done within his chosen field. This is supported by such studies as those of Barron (1954), who found that graduate students rated most highly on maturity of personality by their teachers seemed to be particularly good at organising their work, at judging themselves and others, and at resisting stress. They also seemed to be high on integrity, and to be energetic, adaptable, resourceful, and well adjusted.

Allport recognises the need for a definition of maturity which takes into account these questions of value and, in summarising the views of a number of psychologists on the subject, he suggests that the mature personality manifests the following qualities:

1 *An extended sense of self*, that allows him to transcend the self-centredness of childhood, and to identify with the concerns and problems of others.

2 *A warm relationship with others*, that allows him to love them for their own sakes as well as for his own.

3 *Emotional security*, that allows him to withstand the problems and fears of daily life.

4 *Self-insight*, that allows him to laugh at himself without loss of self-esteem. (There is *some* correlation between self-insight and intelligence, though the one by no means necessarily implies the other.)

5 *A realistic orientation towards the world*, that allows him to exercise sound judgement of people and things, and to take necessary decisions.

6 *A unifying philosophy of life*, either religious or humanistic, that allows him to interpret life's purpose and to decide on long-term goals and on standards of behaviour.

This makes the mature person sound like a paragon of perfection, but this is misleading. To feel a respect for others, for example, does not stop him from sometimes feeling angry or impatient with them. Sound judgement does not mean that he never makes a mistake. Emotional security does not mean he never feels depressed or inadequate. Self-insight does not mean he never feels surprised at himself, or never feels disappointment at failing to achieve a cherished ambition. The basic point about maturity is that the mature person is not constantly at the mercy of his own weaknesses, or constantly vulnerable to people and events in the world outside. He has a degree of self-knowledge and of self-control that allow him to make the most of himself, a respect for those close to him that allows him to love them without smothering them, a tolerance for the world in general that allows him to respect the rights of others, and a sense of purpose and of aspiration that give substance and direction to his life.

Many of these qualities may not develop, of course, until the individual is well past early adulthood. Erikson still sees the personality as having to face major problems of learning and of adaptation in middle and later life. He describes these as *generativity*, which is the ability to innovate, to bring in new ideas, and, in particular, to influence the next generation through parenthood and teaching, and as *self-acceptance*, that is the ability to review one's life in old age with a sense of fulfilment, with a knowledge that one has done what one could to enhance the lives of others and to use productively whatever abilities one was fortunate enough to possess.

It is a pity that we can't take up these points, particularly those that relate to later life, and develop them more fully. The majority of the years in a man's life lie outside the formal educational process, and from the point of view of personality growth and adjustment this is unfortunate. People often face major problems of adaptation in middle and later life which education is allowed to do little about. The middle aged mother who finds her children have grown up and left her, the man in his fifties who finds himself locked in a profoundly unsatisfying job and way of life, the retired couple who have more leisure than they know how to use; for all of these, formal education should be a life long process. If it were, it would make this book a very much longer one, but it would shorten the list of those needing medical help for problems that owe more to depression and to a sense of personal inadequacy and futility than to organic illness.

3

Personality theories I.
Psychoanalytical theories

We have looked at the determinants and the development of personality, and it is now time that we turned our attention to what actually goes on in the mental life of the individual while the personality is being formed. This means examining theories of personality. There are now so many of these theories, and many of them are so complex, that we cannot hope to do justice to them all in a book of this length, and we shall have to restrict ourselves to those that have the most obvious relevance to education.

One convenient way of dividing personality theories is into those which stem from an *idiographic* approach on the part of the psychologist, and those which stem from a *nomothetic* one. An idiographic approach holds that since each person is unique, personality can best be studied by in-depth investigations of individuals or of small groups, while the nomothetic approach, though not denying personality its uniqueness, holds that there are sufficient similarities between people to allow researchers to test large samples of them and to isolate common elements. Idiographic theories originate mainly in clinical psychology where the psychologist (or psychiatrist, if he happens to be a medically qualified psychologist) works with people suffering from personality problems, such as excessive anxiety, which makes it hard for them to cope with even the ordinary stresses of everyday life, while nomothetic theories rely mainly upon the complicated statistical analysis of data gathered from large cross-sections of the population largely by means of questionnaires and other paper and pencil tests.

We musn't make too much of a distinction between idiographic and nomothetic theories. Idiographic theorists see enough similarity between people to allow for the development of generally applicable theories, while nomothetic theorists admit to having borrowed some of their concepts and some of their language from the idiographic theorists. The richness and complexity of personality is more than sufficient to allow a place for both types of approach, and sometimes when the two sets of theories seem to be at variance with each other, it is more a sign that they are asking different kinds of questions about human psychology than of anything else.

From an educational point of view, idiographic theories have been most help in providing us with models of the motivational forces at work in children, and of the specific kinds of personality problems that they can develop in response to environmental pressures, while nomothetic theories, by providing us with instruments that allow us to measure large samples of children quickly and efficiently, have given us an opportunity to look for broad relationships between personality and such things as educational achievement.

There is a third group of theories that we must also examine, closely linked to nomothetic ones. These are usually described as theories of learning rather than theories of personality, but as we shall see, this is largely a matter of terminology. They lay great stress upon environmental influences, and see personality as primarily a learned structure. They are of value to the teacher in suggesting a number of ways in which he can help children to effect desirable personality change, and, in the USA at least, are currently having considerable impact upon educational methodology.

In the present chapter we shall look at just one area of the idiographic approach, namely psychoanalytical theories.

PSYCHOANALYTICAL THEORIES

Many writers (e.g. Hall and Lindzey 1970) see modern psychology as dominated by three schools of thought, *psychoanalysis, behaviourism,* and, a relative newcomer, *humanistic psychology.* Of these three, psychoanalysis and humanistic psychology have made particular contributions to idiographic theories of personality (we shall be looking at humanistic psychology in the next chapter), while behaviourism is associated mainly with learning theories (chapter 6). The logical point at which to start a discussion of psychoanalysis is with its founding father, Sigmund Freud.

Sigmund Freud   If one had to make a list of those people whose thinking has most radically altered the way in which Western man views himself, Freud's name would occupy a prominent place. Freud (1856-1939) was born of Jewish stock in Moravia in Czechoslovakia, but lived most of his life in Vienna until he was forced to flee to London in 1938 to escape nazi persecution. During his fertile career he published so many books and papers (his collected works run to twenty-four volumes in the standard edition), introduced so many theories and ideas, and fought so many battles with his fellow psychologists, that it is never easy to know where to begin an account of his work. Further, since Freud was constantly refining and developing his theories, it is sometimes hard to sort one's way through the apparent contradictions in his writings.

Nowadays, many of Freud's theories are accepted in their most literal form only by the most devoted of his disciples, but his influence has been such that many of his concepts, and much of his language, are in everyday use not only by psychologists but by laymen as well. Perhaps of all writers only Shakespeare's work has sunk more deeply into the texture of our national culture. For the teacher, Freud's main importance is that he has given us a new way of looking at childhood that is in stark contrast to the Victorian belief that misbehaviour and other personality problems in children are the result of original sin, to be corrected by stern and rigid discipline. To Freud, the child is very much more sinned against by the adult world than sinning, very much more a victim of the mistakes of his parents than of those of Adam.

We said in the last chapter that Erikson's suggestion of developmental stages in personality development is strongly influenced by psychoanalytical thinking, and this thinking has also provided much of the stimulus behind the research that we have looked at into maternal deprivation and neglect. But Freud did more than simply focus attention upon childhood experiences. He suggested that the way in which these experiences influence later personality development can only be understood if we explore the unconscious as well as the conscious mind. So important was the unconscious mind to Freud's theory of personality, that I propose to make it the point at which we start our discussion of this theory.

Belief in the power of the unconscious mind to determine human behaviour is now so widespread that it can come as a surprise to know how different things were before Freud. Freud did not originate the idea of the unconscious. It has been with us since antiquity. Nor had its importance in the individual's mental life been ignored (Herbart, William James and F. W. H. Myers, for example, had all put forward theories to show the part it played, particularly in creative thinking). But before Freud, to most psychologists the unconscious was simply a 'waste paper basket of ideas and memories which had fallen below the threshold of awareness because they were relatively unimportant and lacked the mental energy to force their way into consciousness' (Brown 1964).

Freud took precisely the opposite view. After qualifying as a medical doctor at the University of Vienna in 1881, Freud's interest in nervous disorders took him to work first with the hypnotist Charcot in France, and later with Joseph Breuer back in Vienna. It was during this time that he became convinced that human behaviour has a source much deeper than the conscious mind. Breuer had devised what he called a 'talking out' technique, in which the patient was cured of his nervous disorders — such as fears, phobias, irrational anxieties — simply by talking about them to the physician, and adding any additional memories and thoughts which happened to come into his head at the same time. Freud was very impressed with the effectiveness of this technique, and as he had become increasingly dissatisfied with hypnosis, he experimented with it himself extensively. Eventually he developed from it what is now called the technique of *free association.* In free association, the patient is invited to report, without reservation, the thoughts which come to mind in response to stimulus words or ideas presented to him. The theory is that gradually, through one thought leading to another, the patient will involuntarily find himself recalling memories of the events which led to the development of his fears and anxieties in the past.

It was the astonishingly complex network of thoughts and recollections which his patients revealed during free association, many of them stretching back into early childhood and apparently long since forgotten, that convinced Freud that the conscious mind is only the tip of the iceberg of mental life, with the more important part lying beneath the waters of unconsciousness. Far from it being simply a 'waste paper basket of ideas and memories', the unconscious is, he felt, the main impulse behind human behaviour, energised by profound instinctual drives. And far from lacking the mental energy to force themselves into consciousness, Freud saw the contents of the unconscious as kept out of awareness precisely because their significance and power form too great a threat to man's precarious socialised self.

To understand this part of Freud's theory, we must remember that he was writing at a time when deterministic ideas were gaining strength in the scientific world. Everything had to have a cause, a source of energy, which produced its visible effects. In the case of human psychology, it seemed to Freud that the unconscious was this cause. The powerful instinctive drives that his patients revealed in their unconscious during free association convinced him that this was the dynamo that provided the motivational energy for all mental activity. True, in the course of man's evolution, the unconscious has become overlaid with the thin veneer of civilised thinking that we call the conscious mind, but the conscious mind has no mental energy of it own. Within the dynamic system of human psychology, energy has to be transferred continually from the unconscious to the conscious if the latter is to function. As we shall see shortly, it is when there is breakdown in the orderly way in which this energy transfer takes place that personality problems arise.

Although Freud remained satisfied for most of his career with this division of the mind into the unconscious and the conscious, in 1922, at the age of sixty-six, he published 'The Ego and the Id', which proposed a new division of the mind into three systems, with the terms unconscious and conscious now used only to describe the kinds of mental phenomena which each of these systems contains. We need to discuss these three systems, the *id*, the *ego*, and the *super-ego*, separately.

The Id. At birth, Freud claimed that the mind consists only of the id. The id contains everything psychological that we inherit, a fixed amount of mental or 'psychic' energy. This energy is in the form of *instincts*, i.e. of irrational drives whose only aim is to seek gratification for the individual's basic, animalistic needs. Since the newborn baby is therefore psychologically on the level of an animal, he is literally an 'it' (Latin 'id') rather than a person.

As the id remains the only source of psychic energy throughout life, man can never free himself entirely from its power. The id is the primitive side of man, the 'dark force' that novelists like D. H. Lawrence wrote about. The id links him, through the long chain of his evolutionary history, with the base forms of life from which he has arisen. Since the id is entirely unconscious, we are never directly aware of it, but it is always there, seeking the satisfaction of its powerful needs. Beneath the reach of consciousness, and of ethical and rational thought, the id can never be other than a blind, unsocialised, amoral force. Left unbridled, its drive towards selfish satisfaction would reduce human behaviour to that of the beasts.

Freud considered that the instincts within the id fall into two groups, *eros* instincts and *thanatos* instincts. The eros instincts are the life wish, and consist both of those drives directed towards self-preservation (flight, hunger, thirst, etc.) and towards preservation of the species (the sex drive, or *libido*).

The thanatos instincts are the death wish, and take the form both of aggression directed outwards towards others, and directed inwards towards the self.

Freud referred to the instinctive drives of the id as *primary processes*, while the selfish objectives of these drives he termed the *pleasure principle*. During the first year or so of his life, the child is entirely dominated by the primary processes and by the pleasure principle. He lives only for the satisfaction of his primitive needs, and is unconcerned for the convenience or the wishes of other people, as many a parent dragged from the depths of slumber in the small hours of the morning by a baby's crying knows only too well. Presumably, if the small baby went on having all his needs instantly gratified, he would go on being dominated by the id throughout his life, but thankfully for the rest of us, he gradually comes to realise that not all these needs are exactly in tune with reality. People don't come running every time you cry, a bottle of milk isn't always enough to satisfy you (though it may be all anyone is prepared to give you), and the discomfort of wind won't disappear just because you want it to.

In consequence, in a process which Freud never fully succeeded in explaining, part of the id begins to learn a more rational way of looking at things, and gradually separates itself off from the rest of the id to form what Freud called the ego. The socialisation of the baby has begun.

The Ego. From the second year of life onwards the ego becomes an increasingly important part of the child's mental functioning. It serves as the mediator between the needs of the id and the restrictions which reality places upon the gratification of these needs. Unlike the id, which obeys the pleasure principle, the ego therefore obeys the *reality principle*. It contains all the child's rational thinking, his sense of self, and all his conscious thoughts. By means of the ego, the child becomes more of a person and less of an animal (ego = 'I'). Freud called ego processes *secondary processes* to distinguish them from the primary processes of the id. Because these secondary processes prove successful in mediating with the outside world, and in seeing to it that the id's needs are satisfied wherever possible, the id allows the ego to syphon off more and more of its energy, until soon the ego has a surplus which it can turn to more creative pursuits such as the development of general interests and skills. However, the id always remains ready to cut off the flow of energy to the ego and to re-assert itself should the latter fail in its primary task of satisfying the id's needs. To put it somewhat melodramatically, the animal in us always lurks just under the surface ready to take over if more civilised means fail to gratify its drives (a point which has been exploited to good effect by many a science fiction writer, to say nothing of such novelists of childhood as William Golding in *The Lord of the Flies*).

To Freud, the diversion of energy from the id to the ego is the major dynamic event of personality development. However, it is not the final event. From the age of about six onwards, part of the child's ego separates itself off in turn and becomes the third system of the mind, the *super-ego*. Let's see how this happens.

The Super-Ego. One of the ways in which the ego learns about reality is by identifying itself with other people, particularly with parents (we have already had something to say about this in the previous chapters, and the whole concept of identification owes much to Freud). In the process of this identification, the child takes over many of the moral precepts of the adults in his life. But these moral precepts often owe far more to the beliefs and prejudices of these adults than they do to reality, and therefore they cannot be accommodated within the ego itself, which obeys only the reality principle. A section of the ego therefore has to break away to deal with them, and this becomes what Freud called the super-ego.

The super-ego is a very important concept in Freudian theory. If we go back to chapter 2, it will be remembered that we said the child gets his idea of his own moral worth largely from what people tell him about himself. Freud would claim that the super-ego provides us with a model of the mechanics of all this. Since the super-ego is created in response to the code of restrictions, admonishments, and moral precepts that the parents impose upon the child, it also acquires parental powers of reward and punishment. It rewards by the feelings of pride that he gets when he obeys its promptings and strives towards the *ideal self* that it holds up as a model in front of him, and it punishes by the pangs of *conscience* that he feels when he disobeys them.

The contents of the super-ego are part conscious, but mainly unconscious. Thus most of it, like the id, lies beyond the range of rational thought. The child is saddled with many of his parents' beliefs, and finds it difficult, even as he grows older, to take these out and submit them to rational scrutiny and debate. Thus often he behaves in certain ways because he considers them to be 'right', but he is unable to give a reasoned, objective argument as to why they are right. As we shall see shortly, if the super-ego contains too many of these irrational beliefs, and becomes as Freud put it 'over-developed', it can cause almost as many personality problems to the individual as can an unchecked id. However, a normal, well-balanced super-ego is an essential part of the socialisation of the child, and the essential repository of a moral sense in us all.

By the time a child reaches the middle year in the infant school, the three personality systems of id, ego and super-ego are therefore in existence. For the personality to remain healthy, Freud considered it is vital that these three systems remain in balance, with a smooth transfer of energy from id to ego to super-ego. Where the balance is disturbed, and where one of the systems dominates the others and uses up more than its fair share of this energy, the result is that the personality breaks down into excessive anxiety. Since any one of the three systems can dominate, this means that we can have three distinct forms of anxiety, *neurotic, realistic,* or *moral.*

Neurotic Anxiety. In neurotic anxiety, it is the id that dominates, and the ego, the conscious mind, goes in fear of being overwhelmed by its dark, instinctive forces. Since these forces, as we have seen, are below the level of consciousness, the person who is in the grip of neurotic anxiety is not aware of the fundamental cause of his problems. He feels his anxiety as a vague, nameless dread, a 'free floating' anxiety that persists even when his outer life is devoid of any real pressures. Neurotic anxiety is, in a deep sense, a fear of one's own drives and impulses, a fear of losing control over the beast inside one.

The causes of neurotic anxiety are complex, but basically they boil down to the fact that the child is not helped by those around him to recognise and come to terms with his instincts. Throughout life, there is a part of him that remains a stranger to the rest of him, and he lives a kind of Jekyll and Hyde existence, forever on the brink of self-made catastrophe. Should he give way to his id, we get what Freud called *the acting out of impulses*, as when an apparently docile and well controlled child has a fearsome outburst of rage, or a respectable middle aged lady goes on a shop-lifting spree. Far from helping the person concerned, acting out of impulses usually makes things much worse for him. He confesses afterwards to not knowing what came over him, and in the future he goes in dread lest the same thing should happen again.

Realistic Anxiety. Realistic anxiety occurs when the ego dominates, though what happens here is not that the ego itself poses a threat, but that it is faced with so many real difficulties and terrors in the external world that it requires an undue share of psychic energy to deal with them. The person beset with realistic anxiety has little energy left to enjoy the pleasures of the id — e.g. in extreme cases he may be unable to eat or to show a normal sex drive — or to devote to super-ego demands such as the welfare of others.

Extra strong examples of realistic anxiety were termed by Freud *traumas*, and usually take the form of brutal emotional shocks or frightening experiences, but realistic anxiety is also caused in children by such things as excessive demands for academic success or standards of behaviour, by a background of domestic strife, or even by the uncertainties of having to start a new school or work with a new teacher.

Moral Anxiety. If the super-ego dominates, we get what Freud called moral anxiety, an anxiety in which the individual is trapped in an over-rigid value system taken over from his parents. If it is the ego-ideal side of the super-ego that dominates, the individual is excessively high-minded and perfectionist, prompted by lofty ideals which have more to do with an unrealistic 'virtue' than with truth and compassion. If it is the conscience that dominates, he is compulsively on his guard against anything that might arouse his feelings of guilt, and he rejects both the pleasure principle of the id and the reality principle of the ego and inhabits instead an unreal world of taboos and forbidden things.

Both in children and in adults, guilt feelings in the person who suffers from moral anxiety can be so threatening that whenever he has done something which he conceives as wrong, he will actively seek punishment in order to reduce them. Where punishment is not forthcoming, he will often torture himself with feelings of unworthiness and inadequacy, sometimes even developing ritualistic gestures such as excessive ('compulsive') handwashing in order to symbolically rid himself of them.

Ego Defence Mechanisms. Although these three forms of anxiety stem from different systems within the personality, it is possible for the same person to experience all three of them at once. But whether he experiences one or all three, it is always the ego that does the experiencing. The id and the super-ego can cause anxiety, but they never suffer it themselves. It is the ego, with its conscious processes, that is the battlefield upon which the personality fights out its civil war. And whenever the ego is weakened by one of the three forms of anxiety, it has less psychic energy left to fight a possible battle against one of the other two. Thus to take up again our example of the normally well-controlled child who suddenly surprises us all with his temper tantrum, it may be that he has recently suffered a bout of realistic anxiety, such as the break-up of his parents' marriage, which draws off so much of his psychic energy that he is unable to maintain his customary defence against his ever-present neurotic anxiety. The id breaks through these defences, and the child behaves in what seems an utterly uncharacteristic way.

It is fair to point out at this juncture that in all three forms of anxiety, there may be no obvious symptoms to the onlooker right up until the moment of breakdown. The individual may control his anxiety so well that it is not until the ego is suddenly overwhelmed by having to fight a battle on yet another front that we get any idea of the pressures he has been under. But of course the better we know people, the more sensitive we should be to these things.

Freud considered that the ego possesses certain weapons which it can use in its fights to retain control over the personality. These weapons he termed *ego defence mechanisms.* We all of us unwittingly develop them to some extent in childhood, but they require a great amount of psychic energy to maintain, and normally as we grow older we develop more rational ways of coping with ourselves. Where we fail to do so, we tie up so much energy in ego defence mechanisms that little is left for more productive activity. Chief amongst these mechanisms are:

Repression. The ego tries to blot out the cause of the anxiety, to put it out of the conscious mind altogether. Repression is one of the commonest defence mechanisms, but its short-coming is that repressed material is not really forgotten at all, but merely sinks down into the id, serving to charge the latter more fully with energy than ever, making neurotic anxiety even more likely. The example of the child losing his temper that we gave above would be an instance of repressed material, in this case aggression, suddenly flooding back to take control of conscious behaviour. Repressions can also come back in disguised form, as when a child's repressed hatred of a sibling shows itself in antagonism towards the things at which the other excels.

Projection. The ego attributes to other people those urges — and failings — which it is fearful of recognising in itself. Thus the child who is hostile to others escapes this hostility by claiming it is the other children who are always against him; or the person who is afraid of speaking out avoids admitting it by constantly haranguing others for their silence.

Rationalisation. The ego advances an apparently reasonable argument to explain away something that it finds too painful if explained truthfully. Thus a sadistic adult may rationalise his use of corporal punishment by insisting it is for the good of the child.

Reaction Formation. The ego defends against one of the id's urges by placing an intense emphasis upon its opposite. Reaction formation is used particularly when this urge outrages the super-ego, thus causing moral anxiety. The child, for example, who feels hatred for his parents may become an excessively dutiful and apparently loving son. Or the person who has a strong sex drive may become an anti-pornography campaigner. Reaction formation is always distinguishable from genuine emotion by the fact that it is *exaggerated.*

Regression. The ego regresses to a form of behaviour that was successful in gaining attention and sympathy, and thus in lowering anxiety, in the past. Thus a child who feels threatened by the arrival of a new baby may revert to babyish behaviour himself, or a child who is unhappy in a new school may revert to tearful, over-dependent behaviour at home.

Compensation. For one of the id's drives that cannot be satisfied, the ego substitutes one that can. The adolescent, for example, who fails to attract the opposite sex, may compensate by over-eating. Closely allied to compensation is *sublimation,* when the ego directs frustrated energy into higher cultural goals (Freud saw much artistic activity as examples of sublimation).

Various other ego defence mechanisms have been recognised as important since the time of Freud, many of them instantly recognisable to the teacher. We have already looked at one of these in chapter 2, when we said that a child who is unsuccessful in school may protect his self-esteem (which is part of the ego) by rejecting the standards that the school sets. Another child may protect self-esteem by withdrawing from anything that has to do with competition, or may make the excuse of imagined illness (hypochondria, as this process is called, may also be an example of attention-seeking behaviour in a child who feels himself to be neglected). Another form of defence may be excessive cynicism, or a hyper-critical attitude towards the efforts of others.

Normal Development. From what we have said already, it should be clear that Freud saw normal development as taking place when the id, the ego, and the super-ego are in a state of balance, and when the ego defence mechanisms are being steadily replaced by more mature and efficient ways of dealing with one's problems. As normal development progresses, the individual also outgrows excessive dependence upon the primitive primary processes of the id, and learns to displace the energy associated with these processes into the socially accept-able secondary processes of the ego. This *displacement*, according to Freud, explains all the interests, attitudes, and aspirations of the mature personality. Through orderly displacement, the id's drives are channelled into the developmental stages proposed by Erikson (chapter 2), aggressive drives becoming, for example, autonomy, determination, and leadership, while self-preservation drives become industry and competence, and the libido drive becomes marriage and parenthood.

One of the best known, and most controversial, aspects of Freudian theory is that this normal development proceeds through a number of what are called psychosexual stages, during each of which the instinctive drives that have to be displaced and socialised are centred on a separate erogenous zone of the body, and the individual is therefore maximally sensitive to experiences associated with it (the so-called oral, anal, and genital phases). Perhaps because of its frank treatment of the sex drive, this part of Freud's work always attracts great interest, but it is of doubtful relevance to education. Few psychologists would accept it as a very accurate picture of what really happens to the personality during the years concerned. However, we can derive certain broad generalisations from it, which taken together with the rest of Freud's work, suggest the sort of things that we must bear in mind as adults if we want to help children avoid the excessive forms of anxiety examined above.

Basically, it seems that we should take care not to set the child at war with himself. We set him at war by making him reject the drives of the id, particularly its extra strong drives like sex and aggression. These drives are present in children from birth onwards, and the child should be helped to recognise them, accept them, and gradually learn to channel their energy into socially acceptable forms. We also set him at war by endowing him with an overdeveloped super-ego, which demands impossible things of him, or fills him with guilt about the drives of his id. The super-ego should contain only necessary social restraints, and by explaining these to the child at the time they are enforced, we help him to keep them within the range of his conscious thinking, so that he can subject them to rational debate as he grows older (much as we said in chapter 2 that the adolescent should be encouraged to talk and think things through).

Freud tells us that many of the things that we make the child reject or repress are not bad in themselves at all, but simply make us as adults feel uncomfortable, usually because we were not allowed to come to terms with them in our own childhood. It is not easy for us to accept that the child may at times feel intense hatred for a parent or a teacher, or that he may have strong sexual desires, or that he may want to run away rather than to stay and face a threatening situation, but all these things are natural responses. A child should not be made to feel guilty because of these feelings. Instead he should be encouraged to bring them into the open, to discuss them and confront them. Only by a frank recognition of their existence can the child be helped to control them, and to integrate them into his developing personality. If he is forced to repress them, they will remain fermenting in the id, denying him a source of creative energy, forcing him to erect rigid defence mechanisms, and awaiting their chance to burst back into consciousness and overwhelm him.

Criticisms of Freud. We have devoted a fair amount of space to Freud because of his enormous influence upon personality theory generally. Rather as, in any course in philosophy, we tend to start with the ancient Greeks and the work of Plato, so a discussion of personality theory is best started with Freud. Freud's ideas give us a point of reference, and allow us to examine other personality theorists partly in terms of how they have modified and developed these ideas. He also helps to provide us with a vocabulary in which to discuss personality theory, since, as we have suggested, many of his terms are now part and parcel of the language of psychology.

But there is another reason for spending time on Freud. It is unlikely that any man would have had the impact that he has had upon western thought unless there were recognisable truths in much of what he says. In this chapter, I have tried to avoid most of Freud's more controversial ideas and present only those that seem to contain these truths.

This is not to say that all the points of Freudian theory that we have raised are based upon firm evidence. Like most great thinkers, many of Freud's ideas are intuitive, a groping towards a theory, rather than a finished theory itself. There may not literally be an id, an ego, and a super-ego, yet these three systems provide us with an inspired model for discussing the personality, for seeing how heredity and environment may interact, for isolating the causes of personality breakdown. There may be many more ego defence mechanisms, and they may operate differently from the ways suggested by Freud, but his suggestions help us to understand how people protect themselves from anxiety, and to understand how inappropriate and damaging many of their methods for doing so can be. There may not be three clearly defined kinds of anxiety, but Freud shows us some of the ways in which anxiety can be created, and the different effects it can have upon the individual concerned.

Freud himself never saw his theory as a complete one. He accepted that it would be changed and altered in the light of new evidence, and his own frequent tinkerings with it highlight this point. Many psychologists claim that this very flexibility is a weakness. They say that because Freudian theory can be adjusted to accommodate virtually any new findings, it is impossible ever to prove or disprove it. Like a piece of putty, it can be moulded to take on the right shape to accommodate any criticisms that are levelled at it. This is true up to a point, but it fails to take account of the invaluable advances in our thinking that have stemmed from Freud. In addition to the points mentioned in the last paragraph, he has shown us the importance of early childhood in personality development, the importance of the unconscious in our mental life and in influencing, unbeknown to us, much of our behaviour and motivation, and the fact that normal and abnormal behaviour are on a continuum. We all of us suffer from some anxiety, from some inappropriate defence mechanisms. Highly anxious people are just a little further along the continuum than are the majority of us.

The last word on Freud is perhaps best left with Brown (1964), who suggests that without knowing all the answers, he at least 'knew the kinds of questions that psychologists ought to be asking'.

Other Psychoanalytical Theories   Two of the most eminent of Freud's followers were C. G. Jung (1875-1961) and Alfred Adler (1870-1937). Both introduced so much new thinking into psychology as to be worthy of far more space than we can devote to them here. From an educational point of view, the most important aspect of this thinking is that although they both accepted the existence and the importance of man's basic, animalistic drives, they rejected Freud's notion that these drives are the only innate motivating force behind human behaviour. Eventually they both broke completely with Freud, and each founded his own psychoanalytical movement.

Jung, the more complex and mystical thinker of the two, saw man as motivated over and above his animalistic urges by a drive towards self-discovery. As he grows older, so, by studying himself and by plumbing his own unconscious through an analysis of his dreams, his memories, and his thoughts, he comes to know more about himself, to understand better his own motivation, his aspirations, his strengths. Unlike Freud,

Jung held that the personality is whole at birth, and only breaks down into conflicting systems in the face of adverse experiences. The search for self-discovery is therefore really a search for the wholeness with which we are born. When we find this wholeness, we become what Jung called *individuated*, and he would have agreed that the individuated man has those qualities which we listed in chapter 2 as belonging to the mature personality.

From the educational point of view, one of Jung's most interesting concepts is that we can fail to find ourselves by being forced by environment, by parents, teachers, and society generally, to create a *persona*, a kind of public mask that hides our true feelings from others and from ourselves. The mechanisms behind the persona are not dissimilar from those that Freud suggested are behind the super-ego, with the child being made to reject much of his true self and to assume the unrealistic code of social prohibitions and conventions of other people. Jung took a great interest in formal education, and saw teachers as of almost equal importance to parents in helping the child avoid an over-strong persona and develop towards individuation. The teacher can best provide this help, Jung argued, if he possesses the self-knowledge that goes with individuation himself, and can thus avoid inflicting any of his own problems upon his class. He should also encourage the child to bring his unconscious thoughts to the surface, not only through discussion but by emphasising free expression in the arts and in the sciences, since this expression stems largely from the unconscious. And in every subject in the curriculum, the teacher should encourage individuality. Each personality is unique, and can only achieve individuation in its own way. Where conformity and rules are essential, the child should be helped to see, much as we have already stressed, that these may exist only to serve our convenience, and may have nothing to do with moral judgements.

Jung also developed, though he did not originate, the idea that some people are *extraverted* in their personalities, that is that they are orientated, probably innately, towards other people and towards the stimuli of the outside world, while others are *introverted*, that is they are oriented more towards their own inner states of mind. These terms have been further developed by Eysenck, and are proving very influential in education. We shall be returning to them when we discuss the latter's work in chapter 5.

Though Adler was not strongly at variance with Jung on most of these points, he laid particular stress upon the extraverted side of man. Man is motivated, he claimed, over and above his basic needs and his drive towards self-discovery, by *social* drives, i.e., by the desire to go out and interact with other people. It is from other people that he receives the major experiences of his life, from other people that he learns how to understand and eventually to control himself. In common with Jung, Adler saw man as having much more say in his own destiny than did Freud. Man has a *creative self*, a kind of innate ego, that helps him from an early age to start making sense of the world, to seek out new experiences, and to create from them and from his self-knowledge a *life style*, a characteristic and unique way of coping with the world that is constantly open to further development in the light of new findings.

Educationally, Adler's concept of life style is an important one. A child's life style determines how he reacts to the experiences that we offer him at school. It contains *complexes*, that is associations of ideas and feelings that he has about things. The best known of these is the inferiority complex (which Coopersmith's low self-esteem boys in chapter 2 certainly possessed). The inferiority complex means that the ideas and feelings that a child has about himself all contain the belief that he is less effective than are the people around him. This belief colours his whole approach to life. It affects his school work, his long term goals, and even his interpretation of fairness, authority, and human relationships. Adler's followers have expanded the idea of complexes to cover all aspects of the life style. We can, for example, talk about a child's negative complex about school, which means he rejects school, and probably through this rejection comes to despise everything to do with books or learning or the gaining of qualifications in life. He might also have a negative complex about sport, or women, or anything else. (Useful as the notion of complexes is, we need not pursue it further as it is somewhat similar to Kelly's theory of constructs that we shall be discussing in chapter 4).

Adler saw the possession of an inferiority complex as indicating that the individual had failed to achieve the *superiority* that he held is an essential part of the social urge. In the well-adjusted person, this superiority means power over oneself rather than over others, and the ability to use this power for social good. Anyone handicapped in the drive for superiority by e.g., a physical or environmental disability, may compensate (Adler borrowed the term from Freud and further developed it) by trying extra hard, and may achieve spectacular success, as when the stammerer becomes a great orator or the weakly child a great athlete. But some kinds of compensation can be overdone, as when the socially deprived child develops into the political extremist, or the bullied child becomes the tyrannical boss.

After a period of relative eclipse, both Jung and Adler are tending once again to become influential as thinkers. They provide a useful counterbalance to Freud within psychoanalytical psychology in that their picture of man is a broader, more optimistic one. Both saw man as having the power to change his personality even into old age, instead of being forever imprisoned in the experiences of childhood. And Jung stresses that man has creative, mystical depths, while Adler sees him as the seeker and instigator of social experiences and not as simply the victim.

Psychoanalytical Theories and Personality Testing Psychoanalysis plumbs the individual's personality mostly through the techniques of the consulting room, such as free association, but it has given rise to a number of measuring devices which are used in general psychology. These are of interest to the teacher because the educational psychologist often employs them when diagnosing personality problems in child guidance, and they also figure from time to time in educational research.

The best known of these tests are probably the *projective techniques*, which operate on the assumption that people will project their unconscious personality problems (through the ego defence mechanism of projection) into any interpretation which they are invited to give of an ambiguous stimulus. This is rather akin to what happens when we see faces in the fire or pictures in the clouds. The kind of faces and pictures that we see may owe as much to our unconscious preoccupations as to the shapes that are actually there. A timid, frightened person may tend to see threatening things, a girl who unconsciously longs to be married may see things to do with a wedding, a person with repressed aggression may see knives or guns.

The first projective technique to be developed was the Rorschach Inkblot Test (Herman Rorschach 1922). The test consists of ten symmetrical inkblots (rather like the 'butterflies' that children make by shaking paint on to a sheet of paper, folding it over and opening it out again), five in colour and five in black and white. The person being tested, who it is claimed can be as young as three years old, looks at each blot in turn and says what he thinks it looks like. His responses are scored in terms of such things as their content, their localisation (does he respond to the whole inkblot or only part of it?) and their determinants (does he respond mainly to colour or to form?). So involved is this scoring, and so complex is the analysis of what it means in personality terms, that it is claimed that it takes many months of specialist training before psychologists who want to use the test are competent to do so. Unfortunately, there is little evidence that this is time well spent. The test suffers from the lack of any real attempt at standardisation. That is, we have no idea how most normal people would respond to it, so we have no idea, either, of how far from normality a particular person's responses may actually be. And we have no consistent evidence on how much connection there is, if any, between these responses and how a person actually deals with a real life problem. Although the Rorschach is still thought to be the single most popular clinical test of personality, particularly in the USA, it seems probable that these shortcomings, unless soon remedied, will mean a gradual fall from favour.

A more straightforward projective technique is the Thematic Apperception Test (TAT), devised by the American physician and psychologist Henry Murray in 1943. It consists of a number of ambiguous black and white pictures, mainly of social situations, about each of which the person being tested is asked to tell a story. His responses are then analysed in terms of Murray's concepts of need and press, a need being a primary organic force (such as Freud's instincts or Adler's social drive), while a press is anything within the environment that helps or hinders the satisfaction of that need, (e.g. a *need* for social approval can be aided by the *press* of a pretty face). The theory is that, in telling a story about each of the pictures in the test, the individual will attribute to the characters in the story his own needs and presses. He may suggest, for example, that a pensive man in one of the pictures is 'worrying about his failure at work', and suggest that this failure is due to the fact that 'everyone is against him'.

The TAT has now been supplemented by extra pictures which are for use with children from eight to fourteen, and for children even younger than this there is the Children's Apperception Test devised by Bellak and Bellak in 1955, which carries its own supplement of pictures designed to test for problems associated particularly with school. In all these tests, Murray's original marking scheme has been added to, and there are now many alternative schemes available.

Another set of projective techniques utilises the notion that children project something of themselves into their drawings and their stories. The Goodenough Draw-a-Man-Test, revised in 1963 (Goodenough and Harris), and originally a test of intelligence, has been widely used in this context, and there are also tests specifically designed for the purpose, such as the Harms Test (1945). Yet other tests, such as the Lowenfeld World Test, are designed to allow the tester to watch children playing with dolls, and to see what roles they assign to them and how they make them interact with each other.

The bewildering abundance of projective techniques, of which the foregoing are only a small sample, must not be allowed to hide the fact that, like the Rorschach, they lack standardisation. In some cases, there is also disagreement on how they should be marked. Inevitably, this restricts their usefulness. We have no clear idea on how reliable or how valid they are, and some psychologists suggest that their most useful function is simply to get children to talk to the psychologist when they attend for child guidance. This is probably unfair. There seems little doubt that projective techniques can tell us something about personality, just as the teacher often feels he can learn about children from studying the themes that they habitually choose in their creative writing and in their free art work, the characters they create, the freedom or inhibition with which they use words, shapes, and colours. These things give information on the children's interests, ambitions, and fears, and on the amount of flexibility or restraint with which they tackle life.

What we do not know, of course, is how much they reveal of children's unconscious as opposed to conscious mental processes. And in the light of present knowledge, we have to say much the same kind of thing about projective techniques.

4

Personality theories II.
Humanistic theories

Humanistic theories of personality share many similarities with psychoanalytical ones, but they differ from them importantly in that they insist man must be studied as a *person*, rather than simply as a collection of neuroses. They also differ from Freud, though not from Jung and Adler, in that they insist that personality is never complete. Throughout life, man is in a constant state of development, much as we saw that Erikson holds him to be. Far from having his personality fixed in the first five or six years of life, he is in a constant state of *becoming something else* (it is this belief which has led some humanistic theories to attract to themselves the title of 'existential psychology').

We have already met one humanistic psychologist, Gordon Allport, whose work we looked at in our discussion of the mature personality in chapter 2. In many senses, Erikson could also be put in this category. But the person with whom we shall start our discussion is Abraham Maslow (1908-70), who is taken by many to have established humanistic psychology as a significant force in psychology with his foundation in 1962 of the American Association for Humanistic Psychology. From this date to the present, humanistic psychology has seen a rapid growth in its support, and its influence upon educational thinking in the USA has been considerable.

What people like Maslow mean, when they say that man must be studied as a person, is that man is clearly motivated by a whole range of things over and above the instinctive needs proposed by Freud, or even the needs towards self-discovery or towards social relationships of Jung and Adler. Maslow criticises the psychoanalysts for missing the essential diversity of man. Of course man is motivated by the needs which they propose, but it is wrong to lump all men together and say that everyone has sex, or self-discovery, or social relationships, or what not, as his *overriding* need. All men are different, and psychological theory must take account of this fact.

So what Maslow proposes is that the psychologist can do no more than suggest a general framework of motivation, within which each personality will find its own niche. And such a framework, Maslow argues, must take account of the fact that history shows man is not just motivated by his own pleasure, his own desire for self-discovery, his own need to establish himself socially, but by all kinds of ideals, by self-sacrifice, by the arts, by the urge towards scientific discovery. The framework which he proposes (1970) is therefore in the form of a hierarchy. Once the earlier, more basic needs such as those of the Freudian instincts are satisfied, man frees himself to develop his higher order needs, and it is these that set him above the level of the animals. The hierarchy, working from the basic needs upwards, is:

1 *physiological needs* (e.g. food, sex, shelter)
2 *safety needs* (e.g. protection from neglect)
3 *social needs* (e.g. social acceptance)
4 *ego needs* (e.g. self-esteem, status)
5 *self-fulfilment needs* (e.g. creativity, insight).

This model fits in well with Erikson's developmental stages (chapter 3). Through the satisfaction of needs one and two the child learns trust, through three and four he learns competence and identity, and through five he learns generativity and self-acceptance. Maslow argues that often the reason why deprived children make less progress educationally than they should (and indeed why poorer countries make less progress than do wealthy ones), is that failure to satisfy basic physiological needs prevents the individual from developing the higher order needs (number three onwards in the hierarchy) which lie behind educational motivation and artistic and scientific discovery. Maslow calls these needs *meta needs* to distinguish them from the basic ones, and would insist that although numbers three and five in the hierarchy include the needs proposed by Adler and Jung respectively, they include much more besides. The individual who successfully satisfies the needs at the top of the hierarchy achieves what Maslow calls *self-actualisation*, and many of the characteristics that we listed for the mature personality in chapter 2 were assembled by Allport from what Maslow has to say about the self-actualised person.

Maslow's theory is an interesting one, but the trouble is that it doesn't tell us much about how meta needs actually develop, or how we can go about measuring them. Many people see this as no problem, and are content to leave matters where Maslow has left them, but psychologists need to measure things. Perhaps, indeed, this is one of their own meta needs. They also like to explain why things happen. Why should one person want to spend his life fishing while another wants to split the atom? Why, to put it somewhat more prosaically, should one person prefer to go out to parties while another would much rather stay in with a good book? And, through his own interest in the children he teaches, the teacher usually shares the psychologist's concern with things of this order. We can turn to another humanistic psychologist, Carl Rogers, to find out a little more about them.

Carl Rogers   Rogers (b. 1902), like the psychoanalysts, has gained much of his experience from clinical work. Besides his influence within this field and within education, he has also had a marked impact upon the fields of counselling, business studies, and social work. His ideas are not easy to summarise in a few short pages, and the interested reader is strongly advised to turn to Rogers' own work for further elaboration (e.g. 1961).

Rogers is sometimes called a *phenomenologist*, because he places emphasis not upon what actually happens in the individual's environment, but upon what the individual thinks is happening. In childhood, in particular, the individual often gets an impression of what is going on that is quite different from that of other people. We only have to listen to the conflicting accounts that two sincere witnesses give of the same event to be convinced of this fact. Rogers is thus emphasising that not only is personality unique, but that each of us inhabits a unique world, a world of subjective experiences known only to ourselves. Certainly we can *tell* other people about these experiences, but although they may nod their heads, there is no knowing that they understand them in quite the way that we do.

Rogers calls this subjective world that we each inhabit our *phenomenal field*. Like Freud, he accepts that this field contains conscious and unconscious factors. The conscious mind deals mainly with experiences that can be symbolised (that is put into language, talked about, understood), while the unconscious deals with those that cannot (e.g. irrational fears and desires). The primary threat to personality, as Rogers sees it, is that sometimes the individual symbolises conscious experiences incorrectly, that is, he makes sense of them in the wrong way. This would happen if, for example, a child interprets the teacher's attempt to help him as a sign that she is censuring him. It would also happen if he misunderstands a number concept. As a result of incorrect symbolisation, the individual behaves inappropriately in the future (in our examples, he might stop consulting the teacher, or he might mishandle the next step in number learning). Sometimes these incorrect symbolisations are put right, sometimes they persist. Where the individual possesses a large number of incorrect symbolisations, Rogers says that he is out of *congruence*, that is that his phenomenal field does not really approximate to the real world outside.

Although accepting Freud's emphasis on the divide between conscious and unconscious experience, Rogers has not adopted his model of the id, ego, and super-ego. Instead, he talks of the *organism*, which is the total man, basic and meta needs, conscious and unconscious and all, and the *self*, which is that part of the organism that contains all the ideas we have about ourselves — all the things, in fact, that we feel define each of us as unique individuals. The self also contains the *ideal self*, which as in Freudian theory is our picture of the kind of person we would like to become. Unlike Freud though, Rogers sees the ideal self as learnt not just from our parents, but as created by our own meta needs, and our own aspirations.

Just as there should be congruence between the phenomenal field and the real world, so Rogers insists that there must be congruence between the organism and the self, and between the self and the ideal self. We need to take an example to show how this works. Suppose, in some imagined, unbelievable world, it was possible to let children do exactly as they liked all the time, and indeed to praise them lavishly for doing so. Such children, however else they might grow up, would certainly not grow up incongruent in any way. Their picture of the world as being a place in which they can do as they like (i.e. their phenomenal fields), their own desire to do as they like (i.e. their organisms), their picture of themselves as children who always do as they like (i.e. their selves), and their picture of themselves as children who ought to do as they like (i.e. their ideal selves) would all be completely in harmony, and therefore in congruence, with each other.

However, regrettably the world is not the sort of place in which any of us can do as we like. Thus, inevitably, we all of us develop some incongruence during our lives. We have to avoid physical dangers, however enticing, we have to study the wishes and the rights of others. The child who wants to obey the dictates of his organism and assert his will over another has to be stopped. The child who demands the constant attention of his parents has to learn that they, too, have lives of their own to lead.

It is, indeed, Rogers' ideas on how we can best help the child to learn to live with some degree of incongruence that contain his main contribution to educational thinking. Rogers agrees with Freud that the young baby is selfish, but he attributes this not so much to the basic drives of the id as to the simple fact that the child inhabits his own phenomenal field. He does not know (how can he?) that other people have different phenomenal fields from his own, and are therefore not there just for his benefit. He has to *learn* about the phenomenal fields of others. The way to get him to do this, Rogers argues, is not to make him feel guilty for being what he is, but to get him to empathise with others, that is to put himself in their shoes and imagine how he would feel if he were they. Thus the child who wants to bully another child should not be labelled evil for it, which may only lead to excessive incongruence between his organism (which perhaps genuinely wants to assert itself at school to make up for the bullying it receives at home) and his self (which if it wants to avoid the label of evil now has to convince itself it doesn't really want to bully after all). Instead, he should be reminded that within his own phenomenal field he has a dislike of being bullied, and that other children have the same kind of dislike. Other children, in fact, feel pain and fear and so on just as much as he does.

This, of course, makes considerable demands upon the teacher. It is much easier to call a child naughty than to explain to him the feelings of others. But as we saw when we were discussing self-esteem in chapter 2, labels such as naughty or evil become incorporated by the child into his picture of himself. If he collects too many of these labels, Rogers argues that he begins to see the wishes of his organism as a constant threat, particularly if he has a well developed ideal self, and may defend against them by a series of ego defence mechanisms which Rogers agrees are very much the ones defined by Freud. The incongruent person, the person at odds with himself, tends to be tense and anxious, afraid of losing control, defensive and often rigid in his thinking, and unable to discover his true identity. Ultimately, he is in danger of losing all touch with reality, and should the repressed wishes of his organism break through into consciousness, he may lose all sense of self and suffer a complete personality breakdown.

The congruent person, on the other hand, is able to develop (i.e. to actualise himself) along the lines laid down for him by inheritance. He becomes, in other words, the person his inheritance 'intended' him to be. Freed from internal conflict, he is able to turn his attentions outwards, to empathise with other people, to enjoy art and beauty, to interest himself in science. Through this broadening of the personality he comes to experience the satisfaction to be gained from serving and helping others, from creating things, from improving the quality of life generally. Because he inhabits his own phenomenal field, with his own unique genetic endowment, the way in which he does all these things, the way in which he acquires and expresses interests, will be unique to himself.

In addition to helping the child to understand and empathise with others, it is essential to his development of congruence that we show the same empathy to him. This is all part and parcel of the child's need for the positive regard of the adults in his life, for their love and approval. Rogers claims this is one of the strongest needs that he has found in the organism. (Significantly it does not appear at all amongst Freud's major instincts.) It is this need that makes the child obey teachers and parents, even when this obedience means foregoing other organismic wishes. Much of the child's self, and of his ideal self, is formed in response to the need to gain and to keep this positive regard. Where the regard is only given to him conditionally, and there is the constant threat of its being withdrawn as punishment for bad behaviour, the child will sacrifice more and more of his organismic wishes in order to retain it, and thus will become more and more incongruent. We made reference to this point when we were discussing self-esteem in chapter 2. No child is likely to experience satisfactory personality development if he goes in constant fear that the adults in his life are ready to turn their feelings for him on and off like a tap.

Rogers' insistence upon this point, and upon the uniqueness of each person's phenomenal field, is evident in the techniques of psychotherapy and of counselling that he has developed. Psychotherapy (the treatment of people with extreme personality problems) belongs, like psychoanalytical techniques, to clinical psychology, but counselling is used widely within education, albeit by specialist counsellors rather than by teachers. Rogers' methods of counselling are known as *client centred* (e.g. Rogers 1957) because the emphasis is upon the client working out the solutions to his own problems, in the atmosphere of positive regard and empathic understanding that the counsellor offers him, rather than upon the counsellor acting as an authority figure and telling the client what he should and should not do. Because each client is unique, there can be no ready made formula to offer him, as sometimes happens in the forms of counselling that have derived from psychoanalytical theories. The fact that the counsellor is prepared to listen to the client, to accept him for what he is, to prompt him gently when he has difficulties in expressing himself, to approve of his attempts at dealing with his problems, to show understanding (though not weakness) over his incongruences, and to be generally non-judgemental and encouraging, is what counts, says Rogers, and the warmth and friendliness of the Rogerian therapist and counsellor is often in marked contrast to the more remote, objective approach of the Freudian.

Even in the most hardened child, Rogers claims, the need for positive regard is still there. The experienced teacher can usually spot the form this need takes, and use it sympathetically to increase the child's socialisation and academic motivation. However, Rogers has shown that a technique called Q-sorting, originally introduced by Stevenson in 1953, is a useful adjunct in exploring this and other aspects of the child's phenomenal field.

In Q-sorting, we prepare a number of cards, each with a self-descriptive statement such as 'I work hard', 'I am popular', and we ask the child to sort them into a number of piles, ranging from a pile which contains the descriptions that are 'most like me' down to the pile which contains those that are 'least like me'. The number of cards which a child can place in any one pile is usually restricted, so that we get a fair spread across the piles (often a normal distribution is used, with most cards in the middle piles tapering off to least cards in the two extremes). The number of cards is not critical, but for secondary school children twenty-five to fifty cards, and five to seven piles, is about right.

Q-sorting gives us a useful picture of how the child views himself, and of course we can repeat the process, using different cards, for any part of his phenomenal field that we wish to explore (e.g. 'my work', 'my ideal person').

Another, even more versatile test is Osgood's semantic differential (Osgood et al 1957). When employing the test, we write a concept at the head of a sheet of paper (e.g. 'the person I am'), and then list below it adjectives that might define this concept, together with their opposites:

strong	___ :	___ :	___ :	___ :	___ :	___ :	___ : weak
sad	___ :	___ :	___ :	___ :	___ :	___ :	___ : happy
honest	___ :	___ :	___ :	___ :	___ :	___ :	___ : dishonest
cruel	___ :	___ :	___ :	___ :	___ :	___ :	___ : kind
active	___ :	___ :	___ :	___ :	___ :	___ :	___ : passive

The child is asked to rate himself on the seven point scale for each adjective. For example, if he thinks he scores full marks for 'strong' he would put a cross nearest to strong and furthest from 'weak'. At the end of the exercise, we have a useful profile of the child's self-concept. We could then ask him to repeat the process, but this time rating not himself but 'the person I would like to be', and we could look for correlations between the two profiles to examine how much congruence there is between the child's self and ideal self. Or we could rate the child ourselves, to see how much congruence there is between another person's picture of the child and his own view.

As with Q-sorting, the semantic differential can be used to explore any aspect of the child's phenomenal field. But it is time now to leave these tests and our discussion of Rogers, and to look at another psychologist whose work can tell us even more about this field, George Kelly.

George Kelly Kelly (1905-66), an American psychologist whose ideas have been making an increasing impact in both clinical and in educational psychology, takes as his starting point the premise that behind all man's basic and meta needs there lies the urge to explore the world. We explore it for food and drink, and when these needs are satisfied we go on exploring it — for social relationships, for positive regard, for self-esteem, and in the end for the sake of exploration itself. Man is eternally curious. He wants to find out about the world, and he wants to make sense of what he finds. So far, this may not seem much of an advance over Rogers, but where Kelly makes a major contribution to our thinking about personality is that he claims we make sense of our phenomenal field, of our own subjective world, by forming what he calls *personal constructs* about it.

A personal construct is a unit of meaning, a unit which contains all the perceptions, interpretations, and evaluations which the individual attaches to a particular event, or place, or person, or set of persons. For example, a child will have a construct labelled 'home', which consists of ideas and memories of what his home looks like, of the people who live there, of the activities that go on there, of the attitudes it arouses in him. Similarly, he holds constructs of 'school', of 'friends', of 'maths.', of 'stamp collecting' and so on. Because of its perceptual content, and because of the personal memories that it contains, a construct is rather more all-embracing than a concept. By means of our constructs, we understand the present and we are able to predict the future. Without constructs, we would literally have to start afresh each day, and learn about the world all over again. But because each person inhabits his own subjective world, we each build up constructs that are unique to ourselves. No two people ever share an identical construct.

We can see how this works if we go back to the point we made a few pages ago about two sincere witnesses giving conflicting accounts of the same event. Suppose the event is a playground fight, and a teacher is listening with some impatience to varying accounts of who started it and who got hurt most. Kelly would say the varying accounts are caused by the fact that the witnesses hold different constructs of the participants, of the desirability of fighting, of the sanctity of the school rule which the participants may be breaking, of the headmaster who will any moment emerge from his study to deal out retribution, and so on. The older we become, the better we are able to sort out which constructs are relevant to any particular happening, but we still see the world through our own eyes, and not through anyone else's.

Construct theory can also help explain the effectiveness with which a child learns and remembers. When he tackles any work in geography, for example, he brings to the task not only innate ability but also his construct 'geography', which will include all the geography teachers he has known, his attitude to other countries and races, the time it usually takes him to do his geography homework, the people he sits near in geography, the pleasantness of the geography room and much more besides. If this construct is on the whole a favourable one, then his motivation to explore geography will be high.

Many of the items that go to make up 'geography' will also be a part of other constructs as well. The child will have constructs of 'teachers', of 'books', of 'homework', of 'people I sit near' and so on, and the favourability or otherwise of these constructs will all inevitably influence 'geography'. As the construct 'geography' becomes stronger though, so it will place more and more of a stamp on its own constituent elements. 'Geography teacher' will become dislodged from the construct 'teachers', and will come to belong more and more to the construct 'geography'. Thus when the child comes to hear the term 'geography teacher' mentioned, he may react to it more positively than he will, say, to the term 'history teacher'.

Kelly (1955) lists a number of categories into which constructs can fall. Some of the most important of these are:

Impermeable constructs, that are relatively resistant to change, e.g. those formed a long time ago like 'my early childhood'.

Broad constructs, that can be widely applied, e.g. 'all pop music is awful'.

Constricted constructs, that can only be applied narrowly, e.g. 'the only subject I like is English'.

Core constructs, that refer to ourselves and maintain our identity.

Tight constructs, that are prone to collapse altogether if you tinker with them, like scientific laws.

Loose constructs, that vary dependent upon the situation, e.g. 'a summer day can be wet or dry'.

Obviously, some constructs can belong to more than one category, as for example many of our core constructs.

Kelly considers that personality problems arise when an individual's constructs are inadequate to help him predict what is going to happen next. *This* is the reason, says Kelly, why it is so important to treat children with consistency. If we fail to do so, their constructs become a confused and contradictory mess, and it is no wonder that they suffer from incongruence. What kind of construct can a child have of 'teacher' or of 'justice' or of 'honesty' or of 'trust' or of any of these things if one day his teacher praises him, the next punishes him, and the next ignores him for behaviour which, in his own eyes, does not really vary that much? The world becomes as confusing for him as it would for us if one day potatoes satisfied us and the next made us hungry.

Kelly expresses impatience with the fact that modern psychology has tended to fragment itself into separate topics like 'learning', 'motivation', 'memory' and so on. This is contrary, he claims, to the humanistic view that man should be treated as a person. Our mental life isn't broken up into these various categories. We function, normally at least, as a psychological unit. One of the values of construct theory, he claims, is that it allows psychology to avoid this fragmentation. The individual's behaviour at any one point in time is largely a matter of the constructs he has about the task in hand. Kelly even doubts whether, in education, we have served a useful purpose by taking something like 'intelligence' and focusing so much attention on it out of the context of the rest of the child's behaviour.

For example, if the child is labelled 'intelligent', this will inevitably bias the construct that the teacher holds of him. Research such as that of Rosenthal and Jacobson (1968) shows us that when teachers are told that certain members of their class have been picked out as 'academic bloomers' (ostensibly on the basis of psychological tests, but in fact quite arbitrarily), the children concerned tend subsequently to outperform a matched sample who have not been thus designated. This is of course the well known 'halo effect', and it works equally effectively in reverse, as any child who has tried to live down a bad classroom reputation well knows.

Instead, Kelly claims that our constructs of children should be as holistic as possible. The teacher should get to know the whole child, which means studying the whole range of the child's psychological experience, and trying to learn as much as he can about the constructs which the child has formed to deal with life. Where these are inappropriate, we should help him to change them, using the kind of empathic understanding and positive regard advocated by Rogers. Where the child does not get help of this kind, he develops the ego defence mechanisms isolated by Freud, particularly if it is his core constructs that are faulty. Kelly even suggests that construct theory can help us to understand a child's cognitive development. Though he has no real quarrel with the work of Piaget, he considers that the developmental stages which Piaget has isolated in the child's cognitive growth may be due as much to the fact that children accumulate more constructs with the passage of time as to the fact that intellectual processes are dependent upon physiological maturation. As the child accumulates constructs, more and more pieces of the intellectual jigsaw fall into place, and he gets a more accurate picture of how the world really works. Assuming that he experiences consistency and emotional support from his environment, the child builds up constructs that possess what Kelly calls a *wide range of convenience*, constructs that can be used to interpret accurately and efficiently a large repertory of situations, and thus make the world appear a less uncertain and threatening place.

Kelly's method for examining the individual's construct system is more laborious and time consuming than Q-sorting or the semantic differential, but it elicits information in a much more structured, and probably much more searching way. It consists basically of establishing the similarities and dissimilarities which the individual sees between the people and things in his life. We can explain it best by taking a specific example. Suppose we wanted to examine a child's constructs about 'people important to me'. We start by asking him to list these people, writing each name down on a separate card as he gives it to us. We then take three of the cards at random, let's say 'mother', 'father' and 'teacher', and ask the child to tell us any way in which two of them are alike and different from the third. He might tell us that mother and teacher are strict, and father is not. We next get him to apply this strict-lenient distinction (or construct, since that is what it is) to each of the other people whose names he has given us (are other relations strict? is his best friend strict?), before we return these cards to the pile, draw another three at random, and try again. This time he may tell us that father and uncle are fun, but that the headmaster isn't. Once more this distinction is applied to all the other people, the cards returned to the pile, and the process repeated again. In fact we go on repeating the process until the child has exhausted all the differences and similarities between the important people in his life (perhaps surprisingly, experience shows that whatever the area we are investigating, usually no more than thirty or so of these differences and similarities emerge, and often there are far fewer).

This method is known as *repertory grid technique,* because we display our results in the form of a grid, with names across the top and distinctions (constructs) down the side, and a 'one' or a 'zero' in each cell of the grid (figure 1) depending upon a person's rating on the construct concerned (e.g. mother and teacher would rate 'one' on strictness, father 'zero'). The finished grid is a representation of the child's 'people important to me' constructs. (We can carry out the same exercise with other areas of the child's life such as important events, the school curriculum and so on. Analysis of the grids shows us the nature and complexity of a child's constructs. For example, what sort of constructs seem to characterise the important people in his life? Warm, accepting constructs, or cold rejecting ones? Do these constructs cover a broad range, like 'clever', 'interesting', 'sporting', or are they restricted to mundane things? Do the people in his life generally seem strong and effective and good role models, or are they weak and negative? And who seems to be like who? Is father like the other members of the family on most things, or is he more like remoter people? Is there a polarisation amongst males and females? Amongst the old and the young?

Although a repertory grid requires care in its compilation and in its interpretation, there are potentially few limits to the kind of information that it can provide. And numerous variants of this basic grid have also been devised. Hinkle (1965) has developed the *implications grid* ('imp. grid') which compares

	Mother	Teacher	Father	Uncle	Headmaster	Grandfather	Aunt	Friend
Strict	1	1	0					
Fun			1	1	0			

Figure 1

constructs rather than people or events, and enables us to establish for example what the construct 'successful' means to the child (perhaps 'hard working', 'honest', 'like me', or maybe 'lucky', 'stuck up', 'not like me'). Ravenette (1975) has devised a *situations grid*, of particular value for use with children, which employs pictures rather than words.

To Kelly, the overriding virtue of repertory grid technique is that it actually *involves* the person who is being tested. He is asked direct questions about the important things in his life, and we actually give him credit for knowing the answers. In this it differs from so many other psychological techniques (e.g. projective tests and the behaviouristic methods that we shall be looking at in chapter 6), which maintain an elaborate mystique, or which frequently make the assumption that the psychologist knows more about a person than the person knows about himself. They obey, in fact, what Kelly called his *first principle*, that is that if you really want to know what is wrong with people you should try asking them 'they might just be able to tell you' (Kelly 1955).

Criticisms of Humanistic Psychology   Nothing is more confusing than a book that constantly describes theories only a few pages later to knock them down again. Unfortunately, in a field like personality, with all its perplexities and imponderables, a certain amount of knocking down is unavoidable if we hope to present our subject as honestly as we can. So as with Freud and psychoanalysis, we have to make some reference to the weaknesses of humanistic psychology before we leave it. Indeed, Kelly himself was always critical of his own ideas, and never pretended that his theory was more than just another step along the road towards a fuller understanding.

The most obvious criticism is that none of the measuring techniques that humanistic psychologists use really take account of unconscious factors. Kelly's first principle may be a laudable one, but there are plenty of occasions when people might just *not* be able to tell us what is wrong with them. And of course techniques like Q-sorting and Repertory Grid allow the child to give us dishonest responses if he so wishes. At other times he may be honest enough, but just not be able to make fine enough distinctions between the people or the events with which we are confronting him. We also, as yet, have insufficient evidence on the reliability and validity of these techniques. That is, does a confused or restricted range of constructs on a Repertory Grid Test *really* mean that a child has personality problems? Logic suggests that it does, but we still need more proof.

Turning to the theories themselves, they certainly present a much more optimistic picture of man than do psychoanalytical ones, but is this picture necessarily true? It is sometimes suggested that writers like Maslow seem to be providing us more with an exercise in moral uplift than with an exercise in psychology. This is probably unfair, but the problem with things like meta needs is that they are so confoundedly difficult to pin down. We know that man has an inbuilt need to seek food, and that he will go to great lengths to satisfy it, but it is much harder to demonstrate that he has an inbuilt, as opposed to a purely acquired, need to seek for self-fulfilment and for the deeper meaning of life.

The phenomenological approach of Rogers and of Kelly also attracts another criticism, which is that if we each inhabit a *subjective* world, no one can really know what the *objective* world is like, and it thus becomes nonsense to talk about whether the child's constructs approximate to it or not. This is the kind of problem that philosophers love to argue about, and perhaps we had best leave them to get on with it. Common sense tells us that there appears to be some sort of consensus amongst us as to what everyday reality seems to be about, and the teacher has to get on with his job of helping children to cope with this reality. On balance, the humanistic approach seems to be one of the most useful ways the teacher has of thinking about children, and of studying each child's individual differences within the framework of the whole personality.

The final criticism that is levelled at humanistic psychologists, and one that leads us on neatly to our next section, is that they neglect the social context in which much of human behaviour takes place, and which seems highly instrumental in helping form attitudes. True, they lay great stress on the importance of the child's relationships with adults, and as we shall see shortly, Rogers has advanced numerous ideas on how groups of people can meet together to help their individual problems through the frank communication of feelings and ideas. But humanistic psychologists as a whole often seem to take insufficient account of the fact that both an individual's psychological conflicts on the one hand, and many of his short and long term goals on the other, can be caused on occasions less through such things as his own inadequacies or personal ambitions, than through the daily pressures that are caused through working with other people. It may be, as well, that these pressures make personality less consistent than the humanistic psychologists assume it to be, that even people with mature personalities change more from day to day than these psychologists suggest.

For this reason, we are now going to have a look at field theories of personality. Like humanistic theories, these are primarily idiographic in approach, since their emphasis is upon the individual, but they place the individual within a social field, a field which contains forces and pressures that pull him first one way and then the other. They are of particular value to the teacher, since he spends much of his time dealing with children within the context of their classroom group.

FIELD THEORIES OF PERSONALITY

One of the earliest consistent field theories was put forward by the American psychologist Harry Sullivan (1892-1949). Whenever the child's social environment is drastically changed, as when he moves schools or is put into a different class within the same school, he experiences what Sullivan somewhat theatrically called a *malevolent transformation*. Put with new children and with a new teacher, who have different forms of behaviour and of values than he has been used to, the child has to develop new areas of personality to cope with them. If he is unable to do so, then he may show withdrawal, rebellion, and so on. To Sullivan, malevolent transformations are a major cause of anxiety and of disturbance in the personality, and the teacher should do all he can to help children over them. New children in particular should be initiated quickly into classroom routine, should be placed with a sympathetic group of other children; should be made to seem significant in the eyes of the rest of the class by the obvious interest that the teacher takes in them; and should be put under the wing of other children at break and at lunch time. When he is experiencing a malevolent transformation, we catch a child at his most vulnerable.

Sullivan's theory is a useful one, and deserves more space than we can give it, but it is another American psychologist, Kurt Lewin (1890-1947), who has done most to erect a total field theory of personality, and who is, in fact, responsible for coining the term. Lewin's theory is represented diagramatically by three ellipses, one inside the other (figure 2). The innermost ellipse and the second ellipse represent the *person* ('P'), with the former being his inner world of thoughts and fantasies, and the latter the perceptual and motor faculties with which he makes contact with his external environment. The outer ellipse represents the immediate aspects of this environment (his *psychological environment*, or 'E'), while all the space outside this represents the *foreign hull*, the rest of the individual's environ-

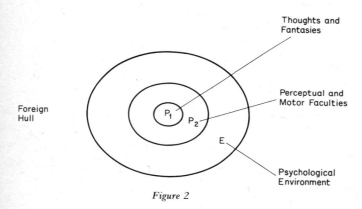

Figure 2

ment which is too remote to touch him much as a person. Together, the three circles are his *life space*, the psychological limits of his immediate existence.

Lewin elaborated his theory to deal with the actual mechanics of how 'P' becomes modified and developed in response to the events that take place in 'E', but for our purposes this adds little of practical value to the insights into depth psychology that we have already gained from the psychoanalysts and from humanistic psychology. What concerns us is the interaction between P and E, and to understand this, we must first look at how E is structured.

Lewin (1935) saw E as divided ('differentiated') into a number of regions, each of which has relatively greater or lesser influence upon the individual. Early in life, these regions are few, consisting of the family and the immediate home environment, but as the child grows older, new ones are added. He starts school, he makes friends, he joins things, his world becomes more complex. Each of these regions has boundaries between it and the others. School is a different social environment from home, home is different from the brownies, or the cubs, or the youth club and so on. Where the boundaries between regions are low, the regions are said to be in *communication*, and the individual can move easily through his life space, or, as Lewin puts it, he can experience *locomotion*. School and home have the same values, he meets his school friends at the cubs, he can be the same kind of person in each of the different social contexts of his life.

This locomotion can be of several different kinds, e.g. it can be social (he can mix with different groups of people), vocational (as an adult he can change jobs), or intellectual (he can solve problems and thus tackle new areas of competence). A *valence* is the degree of importance that the individual attaches to a region (positive if the region is useful, negative if it is harmful), and a *vector* is the force that makes him want to move into, or out of a region. The stronger the valence, positive or negative, the stronger the corresponding vector, positive or negative (e.g. we all have a strong positive valence to move into employment if we are job hunting, and at all times we have a negative valence to keep out of prison).

Psychological problems within P, such as Erikson's 'search for identity' (chapter 2) stem largely from the individual's inability to locomote easily between the regions in E, and particularly from conflicts which arise between these regions. These conflicts are of three main types:

Type One occurs when the individual is confronted by two positive valences of equal force, but the barrier dividing them is too high (e.g. the home-school conflict). The conflict can only be resolved by rejecting one valence altogether, or by the individual changing himself in some way (e.g. the child acts differently at school from how he acts at home).

Type Two occurs when the individual is confronted by two negative valences of equal force. For example, if a child works hard at a subject, he gets moved into a higher set, but with a teacher he dislikes. If he doesn't work hard, he stays in a lower set, but gets bored. If he cannot change one of these valences into a positive one (e.g. get to like the teacher) he may have to reject both of them$_f$ (e.g. drop the subject altogether).

Type Three occurs when the individual is confronted by positive and negative valences of equal force. For example, the child wants to move into the positive valence of having passed an exam, but can only do so by first moving into the negative valence of giving up his social life to prepare for the exam.

The school can help the child with these conflicts in two ways. First, it can avoid setting up any additional ones of its own (we discussed this when talking about adolescence in chapter 2), and second, it can help him to make informed choices between them (e.g. what will happen if the child gives up the subject? if he doesn't pass the exam?). It is also in the nature of education itself to help a child to move freely between the important regions in his life. It widens his horizons, it equips him with intellectual competence and vocational skills, it teaches him verbal communication and some of the social skills. This is really what we mean when we talk about education's power to confer greater freedom upon people.

Research shows that many people resolve conflicts simply by conforming to the values of the region in which they happen to find themselves at any one time. A classic piece of research by Hartshorne and May in 1928 showed that children are particularly prone to do this kind of thing, varying their interpretation of such values as honesty dependent upon whether the context of their behaviour involved teachers or other children. More recently, research has been directed towards identifying the personal qualities of people who succumb most readily to group pressures in this way. We saw in chapter 2 that children who are low in self-esteem seem more anxious for social approval, and therefore are more likely to succumb to such pressures, than are children who are high in self-esteem. Other research shows that authoritarian individuals tend to be conformers too, as do those who are submissive and those who are dependent.

One of the most interesting series of experiments into conformity was that carried out by Asch (1955). Asch asked groups of students to tackle a simple perceptual experiment that involved comparing the relative lengths of three straight lines. Before the experiment, all save one student in each group was secretly briefed to give the wrong answer, and attention was then focused upon the non-briefed students to see what their reactions would be. Although the error involved in the wrong answer was abundantly clear, no less than thirty seven per cent of the non-briefed students agreed with the rest of their groups rather than take on the role of odd man out. Subsequent experiments by Cruchfield (1955) showed that these conformers tended to be defensive, rigid and moralistic in personality, and intolerant of ambiguity (i.e. they always had to have everything cut and dried, in itself a sign of insecurity), while those who refused to conform tended to be independent, open, confident and secure.

More recently Milgram (1974) has produced experimental evidence to show the lengths to which conformist people will go in inflicting pain upon a third person when they are told to do so by the prestigious figure of the experimenter. Some conformers, whilst obviously experiencing reluctance and inner conflict, were even prepared to proceed beyond the point at which they were apparently inflicting severe physical damage.

It must be stressed, though, that in experiments such as those of Asch and of Milgram, conformity to the group or to authority meant saying and doing things that were patently wrong. Sometimes when a group or those in authority are equally patently right, or when decisions have been arrived at democratically, it is equally a sign of personality problems to refuse to conform. To be the odd man out in such instances, particularly if as a result one holds up some important course of action, can be a sign of attention seeking behaviour and of a bid for bogus significance. One becomes the centre of the discussion, one features prominently in people's thoughts, one basks in one's own cussedness.

Besides his interest in the individual within the group, Lewin was also very interested in the group itself. The whole subject of *group dynamics*, in fact, stems largely from his work. In group dynamics, the group (in our case the school or the class) can be thought of as an enlarged version of the psychological environment, E, defined above, that is as an ever-changing field in which each individual group member represents a region. Some regions have stronger positive or negative valences than others (i.e. some children are particularly co-operative, or popular, or disruptive), and individual children are pushed and pulled by various vectors either towards or away from the regions around them. The group thus builds up tensions and conflicts, such as sub-group rivalries and hostilities. It also builds up group norms, hierarchies and pecking orders. It develops group fads that come and go. And, of course, the popularity of individual teachers with the group can wax and wane.

Attempts by Lewin and others to find out which qualities of personality mark people out from the rest of their group as stars (extra popular) or as leaders suggest that these qualities vary from group to group. A person who is successful in one group may be relatively ignored when he joins another. Stars, however, always tend to be above average in intelligence and in confidence for their particular group, and Kelvin (1970) suggests that most leaders have the ability in some way to define the group (i.e. to give it direction, identity and standards), and to act as a source of rewards for group members (e.g. by conferring approval or status).

When it comes to leaders whose authority is imposed upon the group from outside (as in the case of teachers), Lewin (1942) found that the best way to get group co-operation is to allow the group some say in the setting of its own standards and work targets. Once these have been democratically accepted, there is considerable pressure by the group upon each of its members to conform to them. In an earlier, very well known experiment, Lewin, Lippitt and White (1939) found that whereas adolescent boys produced their best work in such a democratic group, they became lost and confused in a laissez-faire group (i.e. one with no real adult direction), and rigid and conformist, with a tendency to kick over the traces when control was removed, in an authoritarian group with an autocratic adult leader (see also White and Lippitt 1960). It seems that by a careful exercise of group democracy, the teacher can get children to show much more concern and responsibility for their own performance and for that of other group members. It becomes the job of everyone to help the child who has particular problems over his work or his behaviour, and often results are achieved which the teacher, left to struggle unaided, could never hope for.

Lewin and Group Therapy   Within recent years, a whole new movement has grown up around the ideas of Lewin and of the humanistic psychologists, such as Rogers, in which a group of people rather than an individual analyst or therapist is used to help people to come to terms with their personality problems. Operating under a variety of titles such as T groups, encounter groups, sensitivity groups, these groups are usually run on democratic lines and aim, through the frank interchange of their members' feelings towards each other, and through an open discussion of each person's individual problems, to break down the barriers which separate people from one another. As these barriers are broken down, and as each group member begins to feel the support and the sympathy of the group, so is he encouraged to probe deeper and deeper into himself, and to bring to the surface those sentiments of inadequacy, of guilt, of rejection, that have lain hidden in the conscious and unconscious mind.

Under a trained leader, who remains carefully unobtrusive, but who monitors proceedings and acts skilfully to protect the more vulnerable group members from a too abrupt assault on their defence mechanisms by the rest of the group, group therapy is now used extensively and to good effect in the rehabilitation of the mentally ill, of delinquents, of social casualties such as alcoholics, and also of those with extreme anxiety or low self-confidence. It is also used as a method in the training of personnel officers and managers in industry, and of social workers and others involved in the field of human relationships.

So far, group methods of this kind have not been widely used in teacher education or in the schools themselves, but amateur groups of one sort and another have mushroomed amongst students and amongst those adults generally who want to improve the quality of life. But this, unfortunately, is one of those instances where the word 'amateur' spells great danger. Leaderless groups, or those with an untrained leader, are likely to do very much more harm than good. Often, through group members' well-meaning attempts to be 'frank' with each other, they can inflict deep wounds upon sensitive people, or strip them of defences without putting anything very useful in their place. At other times, they simply attract people who enjoy a chance to insult others, and who themselves need help which the amateur group is quite unfitted to give. Such groups never develop the positive regard and the empathic understanding towards their members which Rogers sees as being just as essential here as it is in the relationship between the individual therapist and his client. Even where amateur groups appear to be working successfully, they may only be encouraging forms of behaviour which, although they appear acceptable within the context of the group itself, are quite inappropriate in the everyday world outside, and will serve only to increase the disturbed person's sense of isolation from this world, and to make him morbidly over-dependent upon the group instead of facing up to reality.

On balance, group therapy is something that is very much better left to the expert. On the other hand achievement motivation, which is the last topic we are going to look at in this chapter, is very much the teacher's concern.

Achievement Motivation   Once man has satisfied his basic biological needs, Lewin sees him as motivated most strongly by the need for social acceptance and status within his life space (this corresponds to the third need in Maslow's hierarchy). There are similarities here with Adler's concept of superiority (chapter 3). Most of man's meta needs, Lewin contends, stem from the way in which his psychological environment satisfies this need for social acceptance and for status. This is somewhat different from the humanistic psychologists' insistence that meta needs owe much of their strength to the individual's innate psychological endowment, but there would be little point in our pursuing this discussion, since there is no firm evidence either way. Both heredity and environment play a part in meta needs, but it is impossible to assign them their relative importance. It probably varies from need to need, and from person to person.

What is more relevant to the teacher is how psychologists actually investigate the need for social acceptance and status — or *achievement motivation* as it is more generally called. Even more than Lewin himself, the psychologist who has been most active in this field is David McLelland (1961). Using a technique called content analysis, which counts the number of times particular themes recur, McLelland has analysed people's responses to projective tests, and has found that some people interpret such things as the TAT pictures (chapter 3) far more regularly in terms of achievement goals (e.g. 'he wants to succeed', 'she wants to be a doctor') than does the average person. These people are diagnosed by McLelland as being high on achievement motivation (*N'Ach* for short), and follow-up studies have shown that they do indeed set themselves higher than average goals, even taking ability and intelligence into account, and experience higher than average success in attaining them. More straightforward paper and pencil tests of N'Ach now exist, such as that of Mehrabian (1969).

A number of studies have shown the importance of social factors in encouraging N'Ach in children. Generally, high N'Ach children have parents who encourage them to be independent, and to acquire new skills at a younger than average age, who avoid unnecessary restrictions in their upbringing, and who frequently use physical affection as a reward for achievement. For example, Rosen and d'Andrade (1959) found that not only did parents of high N'Ach children give their children more encouragement while watching them undertake a simple brick building task than did parents of low N'Ach children, and give them more affection on the task's successful completion, they also were far less likely to give them over-detailed instructions on how the job should be done, or to show irritation in the event of failure. (Certain obvious similarities suggest themselves between these parents and the parents of Coopersmith's high self-esteem boys in chapter 2).

Finally, McLelland has produced interesting evidence to suggest the ways in which the school can encourage the low N'Ach child. He should be helped to set himself realistic and specific goals, to commit himself to them publicly, to talk about himself in the language of success rather than in that of failure, to recognise and acquire relevant skills, and to procure the support and encouragement of the classroom group.

Of course there is nothing new about any of these. They simply emphasise what we have been saying throughout about the child's need to be helped towards competence. There is, in fact, no real argument from the teacher's point of view between the field theory approach to personality and the humanistic. As far as he is concerned at least, the one complements rather than contradicts the other.

5

Personality theories III.
Nomothetic theories

It is now time for us to turn our attention to nomothetic theories of personality. These are sometimes referred to as descriptive theories, because they are concerned to say what personality is like, rather than to speculate on its underlying mechanisms as in the case of psychoanalytical and humanistic psychologists.

In everyday language, when we describe people's personalities, we use words like 'friendly', 'confident', 'worried', and so on. These are known as *trait terms*, and Allport (1961) reports that no fewer than 4,500 of them are in common use. This is a huge number, and on close inspection it is clear that most of them are really only describing different aspects of a much smaller number of underlying attributes. For example, a person's timidity, hesitancy, defensiveness, and nervousness may all be due to a single attribute of anxiety. If we ignore the large number of trait terms, and start hunting for these attributes, we are said to be adopting a *parsimonious* approach, an approach, much favoured in science, in which the observed facts are accounted for in terms of the smallest possible number of causes.

Such an approach is, in fact, no new thing in personality theory. It stretches back at least as far as the Greek physician Hippocrates (460-357 BC), who saw all men as classifiable into four basic personality types, the melancholic (sad and depressed), the phlegmatic (calm and stable), the choleric (irascible and quick tempered), and the sanguine (cheerful and optimistic). It says something for the resilience of this theory that it was still going strong in the early twentieth century when the German W. B. Wundt (1832-1920), one of the founding fathers of psychology, suggested that the four types could be explained by two basic bi-polar factors, namely strength of emotion (strong versus weak), and speed of emotional change (volatile versus stable). Thus, to Wundt, the melancholic person shows strong and stable emotions, the phlegmatic weak and stable, the choleric strong and volatile, and the sanguine weak and volatile. The importance of Wundt's theory is that it substitutes, for four rigid categories, two factors which can be expressed as scales or *dimensions*. Instead of being melancholic, *or* phlegmatic, *or* choleric, *or* sanguine, a person can now be placed at any point on the 'strong versus weak' and 'volatile versus stable' dimensions.

Whilst retaining the parsimony of Hippocrates' approach, Wundt's model of personality is therefore much more able to explain individual differences. Instead of there being only four types of people, it gives us a wide variety spread out along the two dimensions, with only people at the very extremes falling into Hippocrates' four categories. The contemporary psychologist who has done most to develop Wundt's ideas is the British psychologist H. J. Eysenck, to whom we have referred several times already, and who we must now study in more detail.

H. J. EYSENCK

Eysenck readily acknowledges his debt to Wundt, but his work differs importantly from that of the German in that it is based upon strong research evidence, which we shall be examining shortly. Eysenck, like Wundt, recognises the existence of two main personality dimensions, but he considers them to be more correctly described by the terms *extraversion–introversion*, and *neuroticism–stability*. Since an understanding of these terms is essential for a grasp of Eysenck's personality theory, they require some discussion.

Extraversion–Introversion. Broadly, Eysenck accepts Jung's definition of the extravert as a person who is orientated consciously towards the outer world of people and experiences. The typical extravert is a person who makes friends readily, is fond of physical activity, likes change and variety in his life, is easily aroused emotionally but usually not very deeply, and tends to be materialistic, tough-minded, and free from social inhibitions. Eysenck also accepts Jung's definition of the introvert as the direct opposite of these things, and far more inclined towards inner states of mind and intellectual pursuits.

What Eysenck does not accept (e.g. Eysenck and Eysenck 1969) is Jung's very complex, psychoanalyst's view of personality, which he regards as impossibly elaborated and unscientific. He is particularly dismissive of Jung's theory (too lengthy to go into here) that the extravert is always unconsciously introverted, and the introvert unconsciously extraverted. In fact, apart from his acceptance of Jung's definitions, Eysenck has very little in common with the psychoanalyst.

Neuroticism–Stability. Neuroticism means, quite simply, a proneness to neurosis, to excessive anxiety, while stability indicates a relative freedom from it. Eysenck makes no attempt to subdivide anxiety into three different kinds as does Freud (chapter 3), and remains indeed very sceptical of most aspects of Freudian theory because he feels that they lie outside the scope of psychological proof. To Eysenck, who shares many sympathies with the behaviouristic thinking that we shall be examining in the next chapter, concepts like the id and the super-ego remain little more than speculations.

Measuring Eysenck's Dimensions. As with those of Wundt, few people come out at the extreme ends of Eysenck's dimensions, i.e. as extremely extraverted, introverted, neurotic or stable. Most people cluster more towards the centre. Since the two dimensions are taken to explain all, or nearly all of the observable differences in personality between people, it follows that everyone has a score of some kind on each dimension (Eysenck has recently suggested the existence of a third dimension of psychoticism which we shall look at shortly). Eysenck's results show that these two sets of scores are not correlated, which means that a person's extraversion–introversion score will tell us nothing about the score he is likely to get on the neuroticism–stability dimension.

Because of this absence of correlation, the two dimensions are said to be *orthogonal*, and they can be represented diagrammatically by orthogonal reference axes as shown below. It will be seen from the diagram that people with scores at the extreme ends of the dimensions fall into four groups, characterised as we proceed clockwise around the diagram by extraversion, stability, introversion and neuroticism. By the same reckoning, people

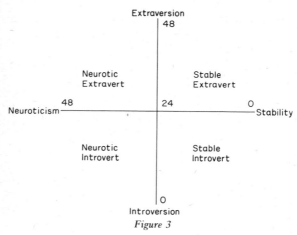

Figure 3

who have *both* their scores at the extreme ends of dimensions will come out as stable extraverts, stable introverts, neurotic introverts, and neurotic extraverts. Eysenck suggests that these four categories correspond with Hippocrates' sanguine, phlegmatic, melancholic, and choleric people respectively (which may make some people wonder just how far psychology *has* managed to advance in two thousand years!).

The majority of people, whose scores will fall short of the extreme ends of the dimensions, will still tend to fall within one of the four quarters of the diagram. You will need to score full marks for extraversion and full marks for neuroticism to become the epitome of the neurotic extravert, but any score higher than twenty-four for extraversion and twenty-four for neuroticism will show that you have a tendency in this direction. The only 'neutral' person will be he whose scores lie at the precise mid-point of both dimensions (though you could, of course, score high or low on one dimension and yet remain neutral on the other).

The research evidence which has accumulated in support of Eysenck's dimensions comes not from devices with complicated and controversial methods of scoring such as projective tests, but from simple questionnaires which ask people for details about their states of mind, and which can be objectively scored. In this sense, they share some similarities with the measurement techniques of the humanistic psychologists, but there the similarity between Eysenck and people like Maslow and Rogers ends. As with the psychoanalysts, Eysenck tends to regard the humanistic psychologists as rather short on experimental evidence. The things they say about meta needs *may* be true, agrees Eysenck, or they may be fantasy. In the light of present knowledge, we have no real way of knowing.

Eysenck's first attempt at constructing a personality question-naire was the Maudsley Medical Questionnaire, produced in 1952, but this proved more satisfactory for use with disturbed than with normal people. As we said at the start of chapter 3, nomothetic personality theorists such as Eysenck have no wish to focus their work simply on studies carried out in clinical psychology, so Eysenck then proceeded to construct a more broadly based questionnaire. The methods he used are of interest. Since Eysenck does not derive his view of personality from elaborate theories as do the psychoanalysts and the humanistic psychologists, it must stand or fall on the acceptabil-ity or otherwise of his research techniques, and we must look at these now in a little detail.

Eysenck's approach was to assemble a battery of 261 questions which a person could answer about himself (examples of these appear on page 103), to administer this battery to a large sample of people, and then to factor analyse the results. Factor analysis is a statistical technique which looks for agreement amongst a large number of measures, as opposed to a correlation coefficient which examines agreement between only two (see e.g. Child 1970). As a result of the factor analysis, Eysenck found a high level of agreement amongst the sample's responses to his questions. For example, people who got high scores on questions to do with friendliness, also got high scores on questions to do with gregariousness, with helpfulness and with happiness. If we go back to our discussion of parsimony at the start of the present chapter, it will be appreciated that Eysenck saw results of this kind as indicating the existence of underlying personality dimensions, and it is these that he has labelled extraversion–introversion and neuroticism–stability (the four characteristics of friendliness, gregariousness, helpfulness and happiness in our example all belong to extraversion in fact).

A detailed item analysis of all the 261 questions in his battery allowed Eysenck to discard large numbers of them. Some of the questions were seen to be duplicates, some showed a poor level of discrimination (a question to which everyone answers 'yes' is useless if we are trying to measure differences between people), while others tended to be open to misinterpretation, or to produce confusing results. The forty-eight questions that remained (twenty-four measuring extraversion–introversion and twenty-four measuring neuroticism–stability) became known as the Maudsley Personality Inventory (MPI for short), and after its publication in 1959 it quickly became one of the most widely used of all personality tests. A shortened version of the MPI, consisting of twelve of the most diagnostic questions, was also produced, and this is given below to provide examples of the kinds of questions that Eysenck has used. The scoring key by the side of each question indicates whether a 'yes' answer would gain a score on the extraversion–introversion dimension (the 'E' scale), or on the neuroticism–stability dimension (the 'N' scale).

Short Form of the MPI
(*reproduced with H. J. Eysenck's permission*)   Key

A. Do you sometimes feel happy, sometimes depressed, without any apparent reason?   N

B. Do you have frequent ups and downs in mood, either with or without apparent cause?   N

C. Are you inclined to be moody?   N

D. Does your mind often wander while you are trying to concentrate?   N

E. Are you frequently 'lost in thought' even when supposed to be taking part in conversation?   N

F. Are you sometimes bubbling over with energy and sometimes very sluggish?   N

G. Do you prefer action to planning for action?   E

H. Are you happiest when you get involved in some project that calls for rapid action?   E

I. Do you usually take the initiative in making new friends?   E

J. Are you inclined to be quick and sure in your actions?   E

K. Would you rate yourself as a lively individual?   E

L. Would you be very unhappy if you were prevented from making many social contacts?   E

An improved version of the MPI, the Eysenck Personality Inventory (or EPI), was introduced by Eysenck in 1964, and this has been extensively used in research in higher and further education. Based on more exhaustive sampling than the MPI, it consists of 96 questions measuring 'E' and 'N', and a further eighteen questions which make up the Lie Scale (or L for short). These eighteen questions are all ones which truthful people tend to answer with the same response, and anyone who gets more than a certain number of them 'wrong' can therefore be assumed to be lying. Inevitably, we must then doubt the truthfulness of his responses to the other items in the Inventory. (Obviously, when attempting the test, the subject has no idea on which scale a particular question is marked, and may not even know that it contains a Lie Scale.)

The EPI is available in two parallel forms, 'A' and 'B', so that it is possible to test the same group of people twice over without giving them identical questions each time. It is usually used for subjects from age fifteen upwards, and a junior version, the Junior Eysenck Personality Inventory (JEPI), constructed on the same principles and containing twenty four items each on the 'E' and the 'N' scales, and twelve on the 'L', is available for use with children from seven to fifteen. A Junior MPI and a New Junior MPI also exist, but are not as extensively used as the JEPI.

Personality Dimensions and Educational Achievement   During the last ten years or so, extensive investigations into the relationship between personality and educational achievement have been carried out using Eysenck's personality inventories. If we take the dimension of neuroticism first, Callard and Goodfellow (1962) produced findings that tended to support the view, prevalent since the work of Terman back in 1925, that children of high intelligence tend to be less anxious than do children of low intelligence. Callard and Goodfellow took four grammar, seven secondary modern, and one comprehensive school, and found the lowest levels of anxiety to be amongst the grammar school boys. They also found that in each type of school, anxiety tended to increase as they moved from the top streams downwards.

These findings seem broadly to hold good in the primary school too (Eysenck and Cookson 1969), where poor reading skills also seem to go with high anxiety (Elliot 1972). What we don't know, of course, is whether low intelligence and poor educational performance is a cause or an effect of the high anxiety. Most probably it is a combination of both. The less able child begins to fall behind in his work, starts worrying about it, and falls further behind still. As we said in chapter 2, failure, like success, unfortunately seems to breed upon itself. Whether our educational system takes sufficient account of the highly anxious child is something of a debating point. The ending of a selective secondary school system should in theory make things easier for him, but whether we do enough to ease the child's transition from the small world of the primary school to the much larger one of the comprehensive (Sullivan, you will recall, would refer to this transition as a malevolent transformation — chapter 4), and whether we do enough to make him feel recognised and significant during his years there, is open to doubt.

It is interesting, to raise again the arguments on teaching method that we looked at in chapters 1 and 2, that Trown and Leith (using the HB Personality Inventory which is somewhat similar to the JEPI) found anxious children performed significantly better on a mathematical task in the presence of a deductive teacher-centred supportive strategy than they did with an inductive learner-centred exploratory one. While by no means criticising the latter approach, the authors conclude (1975), as we did earlier in the book, that anxious children should be provided with 'the kind of support more associated with traditional teaching methods'. And to this we must add, of course, that they need a healthy share of the teacher empathy and positive regard stressed by Rogers and the humanistic psychologists (chapter 4).

If high 'N' scores seem to be a disadvantage to children in the primary and in the secondary school, the picture is very much less clear in higher education. In an early study Furneaux (1957) found that university students scoring *high* on neuroticism did best in the subsequent degree examinations, and more recent studies such as those of Kelvin et al. (1965) have tended to support this. On the face of it, it would seem therefore that high 'N' scores cease to be a handicap by the time one gets into higher education, and become a positive advantage. But a welter of conflicting evidence, using a wide range of nomothetic measuring devices, continues to pour in, not only from Britain but from the USA. It would take up too much space, and serve little real purpose, to go through this evidence in detail. What it tends to show is that the very diversity of higher education makes it impossible to generalise with any accuracy. High anxiety levels in students may be a good thing in certain university and college departments but not in others. They may help student performance in certain subject disciplines, and inhibit it in others.

In support of this claim, we have known that anxiety may improve performance in simple tasks but impair it in more complex ones ever since the Yerkes-Dodson Law entered psychology in 1908 on the basis of the experimental work of the two American psychologists R. M. Yerkes and J. D. Dodson. This could mean, to speculate for a moment, that anxiety is less inhibiting at times in a subject like English, where the student is using his own language, than it is in a subject like French, where he has to recall the grammar and vocabulary of a foreign tongue. However, the Yerkes-Dodson Law goes on to suggest that a *mild* degree of anxiety may be a help in all subjects, since it improves motivation. If we can sort our way through all this, we might say that all students work better if experiencing an optimum level of anxiety, but that what is meant by an optimum level will vary from subject to subject and from student to student. One must leave the question of how this anxiety should be aroused to the individual teacher. The simple desire for competence, and for approval in the eyes of teachers and of peers is often quite sufficient for most students (and children, since the Yerkes-Dodson Law applies at school level too), but there is no denying that examinations can also play a useful part, though for some people they increase anxiety to a point where it becomes inhibiting. It should be stressed that there is no substitute for the teacher getting to know the individuals in his class, and trying to keep anxiety down to the optimum level in each case.

Looking at anxiety more generally, Lynn (1971) has shown that females tend to score more highly on 'N' throughout formal education. This may be partly because of their greater desire for adult approval (we mentioned this in connection with Davie's work in chapter 2), but there could also be a genetic factor at work here, since as we saw in chapter 1, Eysenck stresses the importance of heredity in personality, a point to which we shall be returning after we have glanced at the relationship between extraversion–introversion and educational achievement.

Extraversion–Introversion and Educational Achievement   The relationship between this dimension and educational achievement is somewhat clearer than it is for neuroticism–stability. Evidence from numerous studies (see Entwistle 1972 for a summary) strongly suggests that academic success at primary school level is linked to extraversion, but that the picture gradually changes during the secondary school years so that by the time higher education is reached, introverts are favoured. This makes sense if we see teaching methods in the primary school as rewarding the friendly, outgoing child, while in higher education they reward the person able to work on his own and to produce written work demanding sustained concentration. However, once again these generalisations may conceal differences between academic subjects. There is evidence from other cultures as well as our own that science students are in the main more introverted than are arts students (Eysenck and Eysenck 1969), while within the arts themselves, certain disciplines, e.g. drama, might place more of a premium upon extraversion than do others. There is also evidence (e.g. Leith and Trown 1970) that at all levels of education introverts, like individuals high on 'N', may perform better under more formal teaching styles, while extraverts flourish better under informal (Eysenck even suggests that the setting or streaming of children might best be done in terms of personality rather than of cognitive ability).

This picture of educational achievement initially favouring the extravert and gradually changing to favour the introvert is somewhat complicated by the fact that, after a steady rise in childhood to reach a peak at about fourteen, people tend to become more introverted as they grow older. So, successful extraverts in the primary school could still be successful in higher education, but could by that time have become much more introverted. In reviewing the evidence, Antony (1973) suggests that early developers may be precocious in both ability and extraversion in childhood, reach their extraversion peak earlier than their contemporaries, and be significantly more *introverted* than they are, but still ahead in ability, from age fourteen onwards.

Taking Eysenck's two dimensions together, there does seem

to be evidence that the combination of instability and extraversion, at least at higher education, is the most inimical for educational achievement. The unstable extravert (see e.g. Wankowski 1970) seems least able to discipline himself to adopt good study habits. His extravert's need for social stimulation and excitement, together with his neurotic's lack of emotional balance, make him the most obvious candidate, it appears, for educational failure. Such people obviously need extra guidance and support from their teachers, and would seem unlikely to have many of those qualities that Barron (chapter 2) identified in students classed as high on personal maturity.

The Physiology of Eysenck's Dimensions   We said at the beginning of this chapter that Eysenck shows little interest in formulating theories on the underlying mechanisms of personality in the manner of the psychoanalysts and the humanistic psychologists. However, with his belief that at least fifty per cent of the personality differences between people revealed by the MPI and EPI are due to heredity, he has shown a keen concern to isolate the physiological factors involved. This research is only of interest to teachers in those areas where it throws direct light upon children's behaviour, and we therefore have no need to go into it in any great depth. Briefly, he suggests that anxiety is particularly associated with the autonomic nervous system (i.e. that system that operates without any conscious volition on the part of the individual, and controls such things as digestion, sweating, blood pressure, heart rate and so on), and with the hypothalamus area of the brain that helps to arouse it. Some people, quite simply, may have a more sensitive and easily aroused autonomic nervous system than others. There is some evidence, for example, that ectomorphs (chapter 1) and women may be more highly endowed in this sphere.

Of interest to the teacher is the suggestion put forward by Lynn (1971) that those children who have a naturally *sluggish* autonomic nervous system (and who would therefore be low on 'N') may get a definite thrill from the arousal associated with anxiety (Freud would say this is the thanatos at work!), and may seek this arousal by taking risks that the nervous child would steer well clear of. These risks could be obvious physical ones like climbing trees and rough play, or they could be more subtle ones like baiting the teacher or teasing other children. Since, if this is the case, it would seem wrong for the school to clamp down on risk taking altogether, it should be channelled into acceptable areas such as organised games and outdoor adventure pursuits.

As to extraversion–introversion, Eysenck suggests that the reticular formation area of the brain may be the main physiological cause. This is the part of the brain that helps to stimulate and inhibit the cortex and thus to control the individual's state of attention and wakefulness. In Eysenck's submission, the reticular formation of the introvert allows him to build up inhibition more slowly than does that of the extravert. He therefore can concentrate for longer periods on the same repetitive task. He can also remain more sensitive to the constant, subtle signals of his own thoughts and feelings. Note that the word 'inhibition' in this context has nothing to do with social inhibition. It simply means that the introvert remains much less resistant to the stream of sensory messages that come at him from the environment and from within himself. He therefore needs far fewer of them. He remains satisfied with a good book, or with his own thoughts, or with his record player played softly, whereas the extravert quickly gets immune to these things and looks for new sources of stimulation.

Eysenck also notes that the introvert, again perhaps because his lower inhibition level renders him more sensitive to the stimuli concerned, picks up conditioned responses (chapter 6) more rapidly than does the extravert. This means he learns more quickly, not only perhaps those things to do with academic work, but also social rules and regulations. This may be why there is a significant correlation between extraversion (particularly unstable extraversion) and crime. The extravert may just not be as aware of social codes as is the introvert. Or more particularly, he may not be as aware of the *need* for these things as is the introvert. What could also contribute here is the fact that, because he is less sensitive towards his own feelings, he may be less able to empathise with others, and therefore to be sensitive towards their needs and their rights.

These physiological factors may also explain why extraverts are generally higher on aggression and on leadership qualities than are introverts, and also why at all ages men are more inclined towards extraversion than are women. (Interestingly, extraverts are also more inclined to be mesomorphic than are introverts, another reason, as we saw in chapter one, for thinking that heredity may play some part in the matter.) But all this evidence in favour of inheritance must not make us lose sight of the fact that Eysenck sees a very substantial percentage of people's scores on both his dimensions to be due to environment. As he rejects the psychoanalytical or the humanistic explanation for the interaction between heredity and environment, he adopts instead the learning theory model, that we shall be looking at in the next chapter.

The Psychoticism Dimension   Recently, there have been two further developments in Eysenck's approach to personality testing. The first has been to see which children produce the highest scores on the Lie Scale of the JEPI. Results show that while there is no correlation between 'L' and either 'N' or 'E', high 'L' scorers do tend to be low in IQ and in self-insight (S. Eysenck et al. 1971). The second has been an attempt to construct a personality test to measure a new dimension of 'P' (Psychoticism). Like 'E' and 'N', the 'P' dimension has been identified by factor analysis. Most people seem to score low on 'P' with clinically diagnosed psychotics obtaining a high score. These high 'P' scorers are said to be solitary, troublesome, cruel, insensitive, foolhardy, and aggressive, many of the qualities associated with the psychopath (chapter 8). Eysenck's new personality test (the PQ), also measures 'E' and 'N', and has versions for adults and for children, but it is not yet in wide use.

Criticisms of Eysenck   From the educational point of view at least, the question that has to be asked of any psychological theory is how useful is it in helping the teacher's work with children. In Eysenck's case, although his personality tests assist us in looking for broad tendencies (e.g. extraverts *tend* to do better in the primary school than do introverts) they don't give us a great deal of information about individual children (many introverts still manage to shine perfectly well in the primary school, just as many extraverts do well in higher education). Even if we say that generally extraverts respond better to challenge, and to informal teaching methods, and that introverts respond better to encouragement and to formal methods, that doesn't tell us how *this* particular extravert, or *this* particular introvert will respond. Nor does it tell us much about the broad band of children who group towards the centre of the dimensions, and are neither markedly extraverted nor markedly introverted, markedly neurotic nor markedly stable.

Another criticism of Eysenck is that he tells us nothing about the unconscious, or about meta needs and long term goals and aspirations. Eysenck would be quick to agree with this, but would point out that in the light of present knowledge anything we say about such things is mainly speculation, and of debateable help to us in understanding, or dealing with, our fellow men (the reader must be left to judge for himself the force of such a view).

Finally, it is often said that Eysenck's dimensions are an over-simplification. There is much more to a man than just whether he is extraverted or anxious or not. And again, what about the broad band of people who score towards the middle of the dimensions? It is also possible that these dimensions are nowhere near as homogeneous as Eysenck would make them appear. We have already seen that Freud subdivides anxiety into three different kinds, and draws attention to the importance of the individual defences that people develop against them, and it may be possible that extraversion can be broken down in a similar sort of way. Indeed, Bennett (1973) suggests that on available evidence 'E' contains at least two separate factors, 'sociability' (which may be advantageous educationally) and 'impulsivity and low super-ego controls' (which may not be). In the case of the JEPI, Bennett also suggests that 'E' and 'N' are not orthogonal at all, which must cast doubt on their very existence as distinct dimensions.

In fairness to Eysenck, it must be pointed out that he nowhere claims his theory to be a complete one. He simply feels that it is as far as we can go in the light of present knowledge. Again it must be left to the reader to decide whether this view is right or not.

R. B. CATTELL

A nomothetic theorist who at least escapes the criticism of over-simplification is the British psychologist, long resident in the USA, Raymond Cattell. Cattell argues that his own research, conducted along similar lines to that of Eysenck, and again using factor analysis, reveals the existence of many more than two or three dimensions. On the basis of his findings, he has constructed a number of personality inventories, namely the Sixteen Personality Factor Questionnaire (16PF) which measures the sixteen dimensions that he claims exist in adults, the High School Personality Questionnaire that measures the fourteen that are identifiable in children from twelve to eighteen, and the Children's Personality Questionnaire which is for ages eight to twelve (Cattell 1965).

The terms that Cattell uses for his dimensions (or factors as he prefers to call them) are a little daunting, but the fourteen that figure in his High School Personality Questionnaire, with translations, are given below.

Factor

A	Affectothymia (sociable)	—	Schizothymia (reserved)
B	High Intelligence	—	Low Intelligence
C	Ego strength (stability)	—	Low ego strength (instability)
D	Excitability	—	Phlegmatism
E	Dominance (self-assertion)	—	Submissiveness

F	Surgency (exuberance)	—	Desurgency (sobriety)
G	Strong super-ego (conscientiousness)	—	Weak super-ego
H	Parmia (venturesomeness)	—	Threctia (shyness)
I	Premsia (sensitivity)	—	Harria (toughness)
J	Coasthenia (individuality)	—	Zeppia (group involvement)
O	Guilt proneness	—	Confidence
Q2	Self-sufficiency	—	Group dependency
Q3	Controlled	—	Uncontrolled
Q4	High ergic tension (tense)	—	Low ergic tension (relaxed)

It will be noted that Cattell uses some psychoanalytical language, but he has little else in common with the psychoanalytical approach. His differences with Eysenck, on the other hand, are more apparent than real, since he accepts that many of his factors do correlate with each other, and that they can be grouped into a few broad categories, or *source traits*, which look very much like Eysenck's dimensions, and of which the two most important are extraversion and anxiety.

Cattell's tests have been used much less widely in Britain than have Eysenck's, and it remains to be seen which, in the long run, will prove the more useful. To date, they have certainly produced a much more confusing picture when employed within education than have Eysenck's, and there would be little point in reviewing the evidence since it does not add much to what we have already said in the present chapter. Suffice it to say that when Rushton (1966) employed the Cattell measures in British primary schools, he found only factors C, F and G correlated with educational achievement, but that when the results were re-analysed in terms of the source traits of extraversion and anxiety, much the same relationship with achievement was revealed as with Eysenck's 'E' and 'N'.

OTHER NOMOTHETIC MEASURING DEVICES
Numerous other personality questionnaires exist besides those of Eysenck and Cattell, some designed to measure the total

personality, and others designed to measure specific aspects of it. One of the best known examples of the former, from which a number of the latter have been derived, is the *Minnesota Multiphasic Personality Inventory* (or MMPI), devised by Hathaway and McKinley in 1943. It consists of no less than 550 questions, such as 'I brood a great deal', 'I'm entirely self-confident', to which the subject responds with a simple True/False. The test is an interesting one, because in a way it bridges the gap between the idiographic and the nomothetic approaches to personality. It has been derived not from factor analysis, but from a comparison between the typical responses of mentally ill and normal people respectively to the items it contains. It yields nine scales indicative of different kinds of mental disorder (e.g. depression, paranoia, hysteria), and the results provide a 'profile' of the individual's mental health.

The MMPI is used more widely in clinical than in educational psychology, but many of the tests that have been based wholly or in part upon questions taken from it have considerable application to education. Space only allows three examples.

The California Psychological Inventory (*CPI*), introduced by Gough in 1957, is regarded by many as one of the best personality tests in existence. Sometimes known as the sane man's MMPI, it contains 480 items designed to measure normal personality, and yields fifteen scales which can be grouped under the three headings of *poise and self-assurance, sociability and maturity*, and *achievement and aptitude.*

The Manifest Anxiety Scale (*MAS*), devised by Taylor in 1953, contains fifty items (plus 175 'buffer' items that are not scored) designed to measure anxiety. It has proved particularly useful in examining the relationship between anxiety and learning performance. As we would predict from the Yerkes-Dodson Law, subjects with high MAS scores do better on simple learning tasks than do those with low scores, but less well on complex tasks.

The California F Scale, devised principally by Adorno in 1950, is designed to measure the authoritarian personality, which on the basis of responses to the MMPI and to projective tests such as the TAT (chapter 3) Adorno suggests is characterised by conformity, submissiveness (to superiors), dominance (to inferiors), aggression, superstition, destructiveness, cynicism, and an exaggerated and repressive concern with sex. Originally containing thirty-nine items, the F Scale has undergone some rather ad hoc revisions. It invites a simple true/false response to such questions as 'obedience and the respect for authority are the most important virtues children can learn', and '. . . criminals ought to be publicly whipped or worse'.

The F Scale has generated a great deal of research, and of particular interest to the teacher are findings that in his dealings with children the authoritarian personality is rigid, stereotyped and unsympathetic. Because he is unable to tolerate ambiguity (like the conformist people in Asch's experiments in chapter 4), he is unable to allow children to experiment enough to find the essential balance between individuality and conventionality. Freud would argue of course, that this authoritarian behaviour is a defence mechanism indicative of a rigidly over-controlled ego, and that the authoritarian personality is really suffering from neurotic and moral anxiety. His exaggeratedly 'correct' attitude is probably also a sign of the defence mechanism of reaction-formation.

Support for this view would seem to come from the fact that authoritarian parents (and teachers?) tend to produce authoritarian children (Kelvin 1970). By their inflexible attitude towards their children, authoritarian people may well awaken in them precisely the kind of over-controlling super-ego that has led to their own problems.

ATTITUDE TESTING

Tests such as the F Scale bring us to another area of nomothetic personality investigation which has grown in importance to the point where it is now usually regarded as an area of psychology in its own right, namely attitude testing. It will be remembered that in the definition of personality that we used in our Introduction, attitudes were mentioned as one of the things that render each man's personality unique. We may share many of our attitudes with other people — our family, our colleagues, our political party — but the exact permutation of attitudes that we hold is distinctive to ourselves.

Attitudes can be defined as the reasonably enduring orientations which people develop towards the objects and issues they encounter in life, and which they express verbally in their *opinions*. Obviously attitudes contain elements of value and of belief, and psychoanalysts would argue that we hold both conscious and unconscious ones. Often when we are employing ego defence mechanisms such as reaction-formation, conscious and unconscious attitudes may be at complete variance with each other. Unconsciously, for example, a child may have a hostile attitude towards a younger sibling, but this so outrages the idea of brotherly love which his parents have incorporated into his super-ego, that consciously he adopts a particularly protective and solicitous attitude towards him.

Attitudes are normally measured in one of two ways. Either through a true/false response to a number of statements of opinion such as those of the F Scale (a variant of the true/false response is a five point scale from 'strongly agree' down to 'strongly disagree'), or through non-directional scales such as the Osgood Semantic Differential (chapter 4), where the individual chooses which adjectives in his opinion best describe the issue under scrutiny. Obviously, these tests measure conscious rather than unconscious attitudes, though psychoanalysts claim that the latter can often be revealed if the individual freely associates to his consciously chosen adjectives.

Not surprisingly in view of his general approach to personality, Eysenck considers there may be a few dimensions which underlie all our conscious attitudes. In his *Social Attitude Inventory*, devised in 1954, he claims to be measuring a conservative-radical dimension, and a tough-tender minded one. Fascists, it is argued, tend to be tough minded and conservative, communists tough minded and radical, and members of the liberal party tender minded and radical.

Through identification (chapter 2), children assimilate most of their attitudes initially from their parents, and later from teachers and peer groups. They probably also get them from books, TV, and the media generally. Teachers are often very concerned about this, and wonder at the extent to which children can develop undesirable attitudes through the media's predilection for violence and general lawless activity. Surprisingly, the answer to this is that we are not sure. Bandura (whom we shall be looking at in chapter 6) shows that children certainly sometimes act out the kinds of violence that they have just been watching, but whether a non-violent child could be made into a violent one simply by what he sees on the television is quite another matter.

As children discover identity in adolescence, so their attitudes tend to become more stable, and this process goes on throughout life, so that many people in late adult life prove very resistant to attempts to change their way of thinking. However, in all of us, attitudes sometimes change quite sharply if for some reason or other we find ourselves having to resist things that threaten what Kelly (chapter 4) would call our *core constructs*. This is particularly apparent in research connected with the theory of cognitive dissonance.

Cognitive Dissonance Theory is associated particularly with the work of the American Leon Festinger. It has to do with the conscious holding by the individual of two attitudes (or ideas or bits of information) which conflict (are in dissonance with) each other, as when, for example, a person has confidence in his abilities in a certain subject, yet finds himself failing an exam which he believes is a just measure of these abilities. Since such dissonance is difficult to live with, the individual usually reduces it by modifying one of the dissonant attitudes (e.g. he might say the exam is no good after all). Festinger calls this a *dissonance reducing change*. To bring about such a change, people are sometimes prepared greatly to distort their true pictures of the outside world (e.g. there may be overwhelming evidence that the exam *is* a valid measure). A person who is insecure or low in self-esteem may go to great lengths to distort reality in order to preserve his precarious self concepts and other core constructs.

Rogers (chapter 4) would say that he allows incongruence to develop between his phenomenal field and the outside world.

Once having made a dissonance reducing change, we all of us seek to lower dissonance still further by interpreting all new evidence in terms of this change (e.g. the discovery that the exam syllabus is being changed next year would be taken as 'proof' that this year's exam was unsatisfactory). Festinger claims that dissonance reducing changes are particularly prone to happen when people have taken irrevocable decisions. Thus in an experiment by one of his associates, Jecker, it was demonstrated that a sample of girls each improved their individual ratings of pop records (which in fact they liked only moderately) immediately after they had been manoeuvred into choosing them as free gifts (Festinger 1962). The girls, it seemed, could not support the dissonance of not liking the records much and yet having chosen them as gifts, so they reduced it by convincing themselves the records were good ones after all.

Dissonance reducing changes are also prone to happen after one has told a lie. To reduce the gap between public statement and private information, the tendency is to tamper with the latter to bring it in line with the former. Thus one is able to tell oneself that it wasn't *really* a lie at all. This tendency, it seems, is particularly marked if the lie has brought little significant reward. It is as if our core constructs of ourselves as basically truthful people can survive more easily if we see ourselves as giving way to strong temptation (as in telling a lie that brings a big reward) rather than as giving way to weak.

Festinger sees the desire to reduce dissonance as a significant motivating factor in human behaviour. Since dissonance is unpleasant, it sets up tensions in us that we very much want to reduce. It may be that future research will show us that the authoritarian personality, who as we have seen has a low toleration of ambiguity, takes up his dogmatic stance partly because it removes the necessity for choice, and therefore removes the dissonance which is sometimes consequent upon choice. It could be that we shall also find that people who avoid ever making important decisions do so partly because, through their insecurity, they have a low tolerance of dissonance (such findings would fit in well with psychoanalytical theory). We might also find, in the reverse direction, that people who can tolerate an abnormally high level of dissonance are just as insecure, preferring to be chronically two-faced rather than to tackle the disagreements with other people that consistent attitudes sometimes bring (or they could lack any moral sense, like the psychopath we shall be looking at in chapter 8).

NOMOTHETIC DEVICES AND EDUCATIONAL GUIDANCE

Most of the nomothetic measuring devices that we have been looking at in this chapter have been standardised with large samples of people. This means that norms and standard deviations have been obtained for them which allow us to say how far the test results of any one individual differ from those of the average person. If this standardisation were not done, we would find ourselves asking what a particular score on, say, the F Scale actually means. Does it mean that the person is more or less authoritarian than the average, and if so by how much?

Standardised tests of this kind are of particular use when it comes to educational and vocational guidance. Some of the most widely used of such tests are the *Bristol Social Adjustment Guides* (Stott 1963), in which the teacher underlines the descriptions of behaviour that apply to a child she suspects is suffering from personality problems. These ratings are then analysed to see how far they depart from norms which have been obtained for children generally, and a diagnosis of the extent of the child's problems is made.

Also useful in educational guidance are tests which measure children's interests, such as the *Edwards Personal Preference Schedule* (Edwards 1953). Based on fifteen of the 'needs' suggested by Murray (chapter 3), such as achievement, aggression, and autonomy, it contains 210 pairs of statements between which the child has to choose, e.g. 'I like to be successful in things', 'I like to make new friends'. His results are then presented in terms of the relative strength of these needs.

Such tests can be used in vocational guidance, but they are less good than those designed specifically for the purpose. Rosenberg's *Occupations and Values Test* (1957) divides subjects into those orientated towards people, towards extrinsic rewards (money, status), and towards intrinsic rewards (creativity, self-expression). The *Rothwell-Miller Interest Blank* (1968) divides them into twelve job categories such as outdoor, scientific, social service, mechanical, clerical and medical, and then lists a wide variety of jobs in each of these categories. These jobs cover various levels of intelligence and attainment. Thus, for example, a person whose interests place him in the 'mechanical' category would have a choice of jobs ranging from civil engineer to petrol pump attendant.

Of general use in educational guidance and assessment are tests of academic motivation, of which two of the best are those of Entwistle. His *Aberdeen Academic Motivation Inventory* (1968) is designed for use in secondary schools, while his *Student's Attitudes Inventory* (1971) is for higher education. These tests are really measures of attitudes towards academic work, and the latter also yields scores on study habits, exam technique, and lack of distraction. Like all attitude tests they measure only conscious attitudes of course, and are susceptible to faking, but within these limits seem sound diagnostic devices.

At the primary school level, a comparable though broader test which yields scores on such things as attitudes to school, interest in school work, attitudes to class, social adjustment, relationship with teacher, and self-image, is that of Barker Lunn (1969).

NOMOTHETIC DEVICES AND TEACHERS' PERSONALITIES

On the face of it, nomothetic measuring devices should be an excellent way of isolating what attributes of personality are possessed by successful teachers. Throughout this book, we have emphasised the kind of teacher-child relationship which best satisfies the needs of children, and it would be of enormous help, both in teacher selection and in teacher training, if we knew what sort of teacher could best provide this relationship. In theory, all we have to do is to find a sample of successful teachers, give them a battery of personality tests, and compare their results with those of unsuccessful teachers.

Unfortunately, in spite of vast amounts of time and money, research along these lines has proved inconclusive and disappointing. The three tests that this research has most frequently used, the MMPI, the 16PF, and the EPI, have produced confusing results, with qualities like Cattell's parmia and surgency proving important in some studies and not in others, with extraversion sometimes correlating with teaching success and sometimes not, and even with significant levels of neuroticism and mental instability (on the MMPI) not always discriminating the unsuccessful teacher. Probably the most ambitious of all research into teacher personality, that of D. G. Ryans in the USA in 1960, actually went to the lengths of constructing a special scale, the *Teacher Characteristics Rating Scale*, but its findings that successful teachers are warm, understanding, friendly, responsible, systematic, stimulating, imaginative and enthusiastic carried disappointingly low correlations, particularly amongst secondary school teachers.

Another approach has been through the measurement of teachers' attitudes towards education. A scale fairly widely used in Britain for this purpose is that of Oliver and Butcher (1968), which assesses these attitudes in terms of naturalism, radicalism and tender mindedness. Apparently on all three of these, student teachers increase their scores during training, only to slip back once again when they get out into the profession (speculation as to why this should be is left to the reader!). In his extensive longitudinal study, Cortis (1973) has also found that once they are well established in their careers, successful teachers tend not to be very progressive in their attitudes, and also tend to be rather conventional. One interesting finding, in view of our comment that mature people know when personal interests should be subordinated to those of the majority (chapter 4), is that they also seem able to put the school before themselves. By contrast, Cortis found unsuccessful teachers to be progressive in attitude, dominant, suspicious and aggressive, and less able to put the school first.

One of the main reasons why research into the personalities of successful teachers has proved so relatively unproductive is that whatever personality measuring device we decide to use, we first have to define what we mean by the successful teacher. In a profession that covers such a vast range of skills, techniques and situations, this proves dauntingly difficult to do. One of the ways round it has been to dispense with definitions altogether, and simply take as a measure of success the grade awarded to the teacher on his final teaching practice performance. However, findings on how useful this grade is in predicting such things as future career satisfaction, promotion, or headteacher commendation vary from not at all (Wiseman and Start 1965) to moderately (Cortis 1973). An alternative to the teaching practice grade is to invite headteacher or HMI ratings when the teacher is actually in post, but it is not easy to establish how valid these are either. The headteacher or the HMI may just not be a very good judge of good teaching, or he may have prejudices that colour this judgement in the case of the particular teacher concerned. Even when we use supposedly objective rating scales such as that of Ryans, subjective judgement still enters into the picture when it comes to the meaning of such terms as friendly, responsible, imaginative and so on.

It may be that the picture will eventually be clarified through interaction analysis, that is through those techniques which record precisely what goes on between the teacher and his class in the course of a lesson (e.g. Chanan and Delamont 1975). Thus we may eventually find, for example, that in an English lesson children produce more written work and make better verbal responses when taught by teachers who ask more questions in class, pause longer for the answers, give more praise, and read aloud for shorter periods, than does the 'average' English teacher. We could then investigate the personalities of these successful teachers to see if common factors emerge. Until this comes about, we have to leave the question of teaching success and teacher personalities very much open.

6

Learning theory and personality

We must now look at the contributions that the last of the three main forces in psychology, behaviourism, has made to the study of personality. It claims to be the most objective and scientific of the three, since it concerns itself not with what people have to tell you about their own states of mind, but with what they actually *do* (i.e. with their behaviour). It rejects all reference to the sort of mechanisms that psychoanalysis and humanistic psychology see as underlying personality, and has shown no particular enthusiasm even for such devices as attitude measurement. The trouble with all these things, say the behaviourists, is that they rely largely upon pure theory. Nobody can observe the unconscious at work (or even test its workings as we can with something like remembering), and no one knows for sure whether the attitudes that people express have very much to do with their subsequent behaviour towards the object of these attitudes.

On the other hand, under controlled laboratory conditions at least, we can all agree on a man's (or an animal's) behaviour. Does he respond quickly to a particular stimulus, or does he take a long time? Do his physiological responses (raised heart rate, blood pressure, etc.) show him to be tense and angry, or calm and relaxed? Does he take three tries before he picks up a simple learning task, or does he take four or five? It is these things, say the behaviourists, that turn psychology into a science, not the speculations of men like Freud and Maslow. And of course, as to Kelly's first principle that someone with personality problems might just know what is wrong with himself (chapter 4), they would answer that we have no way of knowing whether he does or not until we have observed his behaviour carefully enough.

Behaviourism was first proposed by the American psychologist J. B. Watson in 1913, and has enjoyed great popularity in the USA and, to a somewhat lesser extent, Europe. It refers to units of behaviour as *responses*, and sees these as consisting partly of innate reflexes (e.g. sucking, crying), but mostly of learnt reactions. It is this stress upon learning that causes behaviourism to be known by its alternate title of *learning theory*, which we have used as our heading for the present chapter. To understand man, say the behaviourists, one has to study the way in which he acquires his repertory of responses. That is all.

Learning theory is much too extensive to be discussed fully here (see Riding 1977). We shall simply look at its main two sub-divisions, *classical conditioning* and *operant conditioning*.

Classical Conditioning   Classical conditioning, first discovered by the Russian physiologist Ivan Pavlov (1839-1936), occurs when an innate reflex (called an unconditioned response or UR) becomes elicited not just by its natural or unconditioned stimulus (US) but by an unnatural stimulus (a conditioned stimulus or CS) as well. This happens if the CS and the US occur close together frequently. Thus if a light is flashed (CS) every time we get an electric shock (US), the wince (UR) normally elicited by the shock in time becomes elicited by the light alone. The wince is now called a *conditioned response.*

Pavlov believed that the whole of the complex activity of man is simply a collection of conditioned responses. The baby's love for his mother, for example, would thus be explained by the fact that the mother is present as a CS every time the baby receives his milk (US). Over a period of time, the pleasure which is the UR to the milk becomes elicited as a conditioned response (CR) by the mother as well, even when it is not feeding time. Evidence that stimulus-response bonds, as they are called, of this kind can be set up was produced by Watson himself (Watson and Rayner 1919), who found that the natural fear which a baby boy called Albert had for loud noises could become associated as well with the previously innocuous stimulus of a white rat, if rat and noise were produced together often enough. Through what Watson called *stimulus generalisation*, it was then found that Albert had also become afraid of anything that looked like a white rat, such as a white rabbit or even Watson himself in a long white Santa Claus beard.

It is now known, of course, that although some behaviour can be explained through classical conditioning, it is inadequate as an explanation of all behaviour. The learning which it accounts for seems to be largely confined to responses which occur in the autonomic nervous system (i.e. to involuntary rather than to consciously mediated responses), and in any case, conditioned responses tend to weaken and disappear (become extinct) as soon as the US and the CS finally cease to occur together. Behaviourism, nowadays, tends therefore to pay much more attention to operant conditioning.

Operant Conditioning Operant conditioning differs chiefly from classical conditioning in that instead of concentrating upon the stimulus which *precedes* a response, it concentrates upon the consequences that follow *after* the response. Operant conditioning theory holds that if a response has pleasant consequences (is 'rewarded' or 'reinforced') it tends to be repeated, if it has unpleasant consequences (is 'punished' in some way), it tends not to be. This principle was originally stated, at somewhat greater length, by one of the pioneers of behaviourism, the American psychologist E. L. Thorndike (1874-1949) in his 'Law of Effect', but it is now particularly associated with the work of perhaps the best known of all American psychologists, B. F. Skinner (b. 1904).

Skinner, in a number of publications (most recently 1972), takes up Thorndike's view that since human behaviour most frequently occurs in the absence of any precedent stimulus, classical conditioning, even if it was not subject to extinction and covered learning in the central nervous system as well as in the autonomic, could not explain most of human behaviour. He also maintains that we should give up the idea that behaviour is prompted by instincts, needs, or drives such as those suggested by the psychoanalysts or the humanists. Instead, we should 'shift to the environment a causal role previously assigned to a person's feelings, states of mind, purposes, or other attributes' (1972). This does not mean that Skinner rejects the idea of innate differences. People differ from each other in their physiological endowments, and therefore must differ from each other in the level of the responses which they make to the environment. What he does reject is the idea that man's habits, his likes and dislikes, his beliefs, his moral judgements, in sum his personality, is anything more than a set of learned responses to the particular environmental circumstances he has encountered during his life to date. Thus the belief that man has free will, or autonomy, or control over his individual destiny, is an illusion.

Over the last forty years, Skinner has amassed a great deal of evidence, working with both men and with animals, in support of this view. The details of this evidence belong more to a book on learning than to one on personality, but we can see how they can be applied to personality if we take the example of a child who is consistently misbehaving in class. Skinner would say that the child is misbehaving not because he 'feels' like it (i.e. as the result of a freely taken decision), but because of the experiences that he has had in his life so far. These experiences have rewarded (reinforced) his disruptive behaviour, have stamped it in and made it a part of his personality. He may be a child with an unstimulating home background, who has tended only to be reinforced with adult attention when he behaves badly. Good behaviour goes unnoticed, and therefore has tended to disappear from his behavioural repertoire. Or he may be a friendless child, who is only rewarded with the approval of his peers when he enlivens things by cheeking the teacher. Or he may be a child who is backward in class and who is largely ignored by the teacher unless he becomes disruptive.

If we take the opposite example of a child who behaves well, Skinner would say that this good behaviour is a result of the frequent and sympathetic adult attention with which such behaviour has been reinforced at home. Where we have a well behaved child who, for example, becomes difficult on the birth of a baby sibling, Skinner would deny that this has anything to do with regression (chapter 3) and would say it is simply because the mother is now too busy to notice him when he is good, and only turns her attention to him when he does something wrong.

Note that what Skinner is saying here is that the very *fact* of adult attention can be rewarding to a child, even though it be angry attention. Adults often assume that simply because they are speaking crossly to a child he is actually experiencing punishment, whereas in truth the real punishment might be to ignore him altogether. By speaking crossly to him, one is at least acknowledging his existence, and, by showing him that he is important enough to make adults angry, one is demonstrating that he has power over the immediate environment. We shall return to this point later in the chapter, but what Skinner is in effect saying is that often we make children's behaviour worse by inadvertently reinforcing it when we imagine ourselves to be doing the opposite.

It can probably be deduced from what we have said already that Skinner's attitude to psychoanalysis and humanistic psychology is a very antagonistic one. He sees no reason for postulating the existence of id, ego, or super-ego, or meta needs, or ego defence mechanisms, or for the various processes that psychoanalysts and humanistic psychologists advance to account for the existence of neuroses. People become neurotic, Skinner argues, because their environment makes them so, in particular through reinforcing them in a haphazard and unpredictable way, and by handing out harsh punishments. It is quite possible to make a laboratory animal 'neurotic' by this kind of treatment, and no one suggests that laboratory animals have id, ego and super-ego.

Skinner is very much less at odds with Eysenck and with the nomothetic approach to personality than he is with the psychoanalysts and humanists (and indeed Eysenck is very much less at odds with Skinner). He would accept Eysenck's attempt to relate the personality to such physiological systems as the hypothalamus and the reticular formation areas of the brain. He would also accept Eysenck's view that a large percentage of attributes like anxiety and introversion may be inherited, if by inherited we mean that some people develop the conditioned responses that are described as 'anxiety' and 'introversion' more readily than do others.

Of course, Skinner does not pretend that it is always possible to point to the precise cause in a person's environment of each item of his present behaviour. The consequences of a particular learning experience, especially in a complex society such as ours, are often long delayed. But the rule remains that all behaviour is caused. Thus when we observe an activity that seems to us to be spontaneous and creative, we are simply witnessing the consequences of a piece of experience that may have taken place much earlier. 'Consequences', says Skinner (1972) 'take over a role previously assigned to an antecedent creative mind.' Embedded in this line of reasoning is Skinner's emphasis upon *performance* as well as upon learning. We are learning new things all the time, but this learning may not be very apparent in our performance until it is suddenly reinforced by our environment. Thus a child may learn to discriminate between musical notes, but show little sign of this skill until he is suddenly re-inforced by teacher approval when he starts taking music lessons.

Skinner recognises the existence of both primary and secondary re-inforcers. The former (e.g. food, warmth, shelter) have intrinsic value, the latter (e.g. money) have not, but have become desirable through their association with the former. In our complex society, a great deal of social behaviour is the result of secondary re-inforcement. Since a school is a particularly artificial environment, in which children have to learn in a few years information that has taken centuries of research and discovery, Skinner accepts that it cannot help but rely upon secondary re-inforcement (such as teacher approval, good grades, examination success). Usually these secondary re-inforcers are built into what Skinner calls 'chains', with each re-inforcer associated with the next and so on back to a primary re-inforcer. Thus a child values good marks (secondary re-inforcer) because they are associated with parental approval (secondary re-inforcer) which is associated with improved creature comforts (primary re-inforcer). As might be predicted from his extreme environmentalist viewpoint, Skinner places great emphasis upon the importance of education, and deplores the fact that, partly through teachers' misapplication of re-inforcers, it is generally so inefficient.

We shall be returning shortly to some of the things that Skinner claims can be done to render education more efficient. We will now look at another set of learning theories, somewhat related to operant conditioning by virtue of their similar emphasis upon the environment, namely social learning theories.

Social Learning Theories Social learning theories are associated particularly with the work of the Canadian psychologist Albert Bandura (b. 1925). Bandura has been much influenced by the behaviourists, but he differs from them in insisting that much behaviour takes place in the absence of any kind of re-inforcement at all. The child, he claims, has an innate propensity for copying the behaviour of others, even when he receives no reward for doing so. Much learning, therefore, takes place by *imitation* (or *modelling*). It is strange that before the work of Bandura and of other social learning theorists, psychologists had tended to neglect imitation as an important element in shaping human behaviour.

Imitation, Bandura claims (e.g. 1969), explains both broad cultural movements (fashions, fads, mass hysteria, etc.) and the individual socialisation of the child. The child's personality is, therefore, largely an imitation, within the limits laid down by innate differences, of those around him. In a sense, Bandura helps span a small part of the gap between the behaviourists and the psychoanalysts, since he would accept the latter's emphasis upon the child's acquisition of role behaviour from his parents, though he has shown little enthusiasm for the idea of various systems within the personality, or for meta needs. As for self-actualisation, Bandura would claim that the child's basic need to copy those around him is sufficient explanation of the origin of many of the goals and aims that he develops in life.

Bandura's emphasis upon the possibility of learning taking place in the absence of re-inforcement does not mean that he sees the latter as unimportant. A child is more likely to imitate a model who is being rewarded for his actions than one who is being punished, and once having imitated his behaviour, this imitation is more likely to persist if it is rewarded in its own turn. Bandura also accepts Skinner's distinction between learning and performance. A child need not necessarily *perform* the actions of another at the moment he is learning them. He can store up these actions mentally and produce them at an appropriate time later on, as when a boy watches a cowboy film and next day at school acts out the role of the hero.

Bandura also considers that the more prestigious the model, the more likely the child will be to imitate his behaviour (hence violence on the football field by a star player is more likely to spread to the watching crowd than violence by a lesser known one). Since this imitation goes on in the absence of rewards and punishments, this means that the child may well be learning many things from a prestigious model like, for example, the teacher, which the model himself has no idea he is teaching. This is particularly true of emotions. The child may have all kinds of emotional behaviour modelled unwittingly for him by the teacher, such as sympathy towards those in difficulties, or impatience and anger. Bandura has made a special study of aggression, which he feels lends itself especially well to a social learning theory interpretation. In a number of research studies (see Bandura 1973 for a summary), he has shown that children who witness adult aggression are much more likely to behave aggressively themselves than are children who do not. It is as if the adult aggression sanctions similar behaviour in children. And of course if the children find that this aggression pays off in helping them to get their own way, then it may become an established part of their behaviour.

Innate differences and the child's own previous experiences will obviously affect the extent to which social learning takes place. Jakubczak and Walters (1959) show that dependent children imitate prestige figures more readily than do those who are less dependent, and that timid or anxious children take over fearful responses vicariously more frequently than do secure and confident ones. Similarly, children who have learnt to respond warmly to teachers in the past will be far readier to take them as models in the present, while someone who has learnt, e.g. to despise the opposite sex, will be less likely to accept a member of that sex as a model than will someone who has learnt to respect it. Similarly again, a child who has seen someone behaving ineffectually in the past, or receiving frequent punishment, will be less likely to accept them as a model than he will be to accept someone who has been behaving with success.

In the next section, we shall be looking at some of the practical applications of Bandura's theories for the teacher, together with the application of those of Skinner.

Techniques for Modifying Children's Behaviour If, as the behaviourists believe, personality problems such as neuroticism or maladjustment are simply caused by the wrong kinds of stimulus-response bonds or by the wrong kinds of reinforcement, it follows that if we want to cure people of these problems, all we have to do is to break these bonds or to reverse this reinforcement. This, indeed, is the principle behind *behaviour therapy*, which is the behaviouristic equivalent of psychoanalysis or Rogerian therapy. It has the advantage of extreme simplicity, and in certain circumstances at least, it seems to work. To see how it does, perhaps we could first go back to Watson's experiment with little Albert. Once having conditioned Albert to feel fear for the white rat by associating it with the unpleasant stimulus of the loud noise, we can remove this fear (in other words, *de-sensitise* Albert) by now associating the white rat with something pleasant. This means presenting the rat to Albert along with something of which he is very fond, say jelly. Each time Albert sees the rat, he gets his plate of jelly. This has to be done discreetly, with a respectable distance at first between the rat and Albert while he eats his jelly, otherwise his aversion for the former could just end up by being associated with the latter.

Similarly, by *aversion* therapy, it is possible to turn somebody against something (a bad habit, a deviant activity), just as Albert was turned against the rat in the first place, by pairing it with something unpleasant. Thus, for example, a smoker can be given an electric shock every time he opens his cigarette packet, or a finger nail biter can have his nails coated with a foul tasting substance.

De-sensitisation and aversion therapy have been used extensively to treat a wide range of anxieties, phobias, and deviances. It will be noted that they waste no time probing the subject's previous experience to find the exact situation that gave rise to his unwanted behaviour. Nor do they see this behaviour as a symptom of some deeper, unconscious malaise. They see the symptom and the anxiety, or phobia or whatever it happens to be, as essentially the same thing, with the cure of the former necessarily also curing the latter.

De-sensitisation and aversion therapy are based, of course, on classical conditioning techniques. The operant conditioning approach to behaviour therapy is somewhat broader. It focuses upon consistently re-inforcing the wanted behaviour, while at the same time, if possible, withholding reinforcement from the unwanted. Thus to cure a man of smoking by operant conditioning, we would not rely upon the, often impractical, business of associating his smoking with something unpleasant, we would concentrate instead on rewarding him for *not* smoking. As long as our reinforcement of his non-smoking is consistent and thorough, the operant conditioning theorists hold that this will be a much more effective way of getting him to stop smoking than by treating his smoking as a sign of oral fixation (as the Freudian might), or by giving him any number of lectures on the evils of smoking.

Social learning theorists accept this operant conditioning approach, but also lay stress upon providing the subject with models of the reformed behaviour we want from him. Thus, to continue with our example of smoking, the smoker would be exposed to prestigious non-smokers, instead of, as happens more frequently at the moment, to prestigious smokers.

All the above techniques, and particularly those associated with operant conditioning and social learning, are now in wide use, especially in the USA. Since they are used to change all kinds of behaviour, and not just the behaviour of those in need of therapy, the collective title of *behaviour modification* is usually assigned to them. Our interest in these techniques lies chiefly in what they can achieve in the classroom, and it is in this context that both Skinner and Bandura have put forward many of their ideas. Perhaps we can best start by taking the example of an isolate child in the infant school, who refuses to mix with the other children. The natural reaction of the sympathetic teacher is to spend much of her time approaching him solicitously and attempting to draw him into group activities. The net result of all this is that often by the end of term he is no more sociable than he was at the beginning. The teacher may redouble her efforts the following term, but with no better results. What has gone wrong? Well, argue the exponents of behaviour modification, the teacher has actually been *re-inforcing* the child's isolate behaviour. She has rewarded him for being an isolate by paying attention to him every time he is on his own. And doubtless, on the occasions when she has succeeded in drawing him into a group, she has then withdrawn her attention from him thinking it was no longer needed. What she *should* have done is the exact opposite, i.e. to withhold her attention from the child while he is behaving as an isolate, and to give it to him every time he makes an approach response to other children. In this way, he will learn that instead of getting teacher's attention by being on his own, the way to get it is to be with others.

We can take this model and apply it to other kinds of behaviour. Just as the isolate child was being rewarded for being an isolate, so a child who is not very good at his work may find that the only way he can get his teacher's attention is by playing about. Another child may find that by showing contempt for a subject he can always draw the teacher's attention away from the lesson and into a fruitless attempt to 'convert' him to a better attitude. Another may find that by using bad language he can offend (and therefore strike back at) a teacher he dislikes. Another that he can get more attention from a popular teacher by getting his work wrong than by getting it right. In all cases, the logic of the situation remains the same. The child is being rewarded for the very kinds of behaviour that the teacher wishes to eliminate in him. Defects of personality, Skinner argues, are caused by a misapplication of re-inforcers. Study the situation, apply the re-inforcers differently, and the defects will be cured (or, more technically, *modified*).

There are several texts available which go into the techniques of behaviour modification exhaustively (e.g. Poteet 1974). But basically these techniques can be reduced to a few simple rules:

1 The teacher lists each of the behaviours in a particular child that he wishes to modify. This must be done in detail — e.g. it is not enough just to write down 'rowdiness', one must break this down into such things as 'entering class noisily', 'banging desk lid', 'scraping chair on floor'. These are called *target behaviours.*

2 The teacher lists against each of these the target behaviours that are to be aimed for (normally the exact opposite of those in the first list).

3 The teacher analyses precisely how target behaviours in list one have been re-inforced in the past, and withdraws this re-inforcement.

4 The teacher systematically re-inforces the target behaviours in list two.

All this requires skill and patience. It also requires self-control, as when the teacher deliberately ignores a child's noisy entrance into the class, and praises him when he takes his seat quietly. Bandura claims that the teacher can help things along still further by modelling the desired behaviour himself (e.g. not shouting in class if he doesn't want the children to do so), by drawing favourable attention to children who are modelling the desired behaviour (but only if they are prestigious models), and by always stressing in his instructions to the class the desired rather than the undesired behaviour (e.g. 'work quietly' rather than 'stop the noise').

It is also claimed that behaviour modification techniques can be used to produce less tangible kinds of behaviour such as patience, self-control, determination (in fact the whole range of the things referred to in chapter 5 as traits). This is done by what is called *self-contracting*, a kind of course in self-management. Tharp and Wetzel (1969) report a successful attempt to employ self-contracting in a large secondary school and the surrounding community. Once target behaviours had been listed for individual children, *mediators*, such as parents, local trades-people and so on, who could provide the children with suitable rewards, were contacted and their help enlisted. Children were then asked to contract to produce desired target behaviours in return for specified rewards. Each time they produced the behaviours (e.g. truthfulness, co-operation, perseverance) they were awarded notations which could be accumulated and then exchanged for the rewards (e.g. extra time watching TV, outings, horse rides, helping in a garage, extra pocket money). Within two to six weeks, Tharp and Wetzel claim that seventy five per cent of the undesired behaviour had been converted (*turned round*) into desired behaviour. The children had learnt, many of them for the first time in their lives, that things like honesty actually pay off. In the course of this learning, they had also acquired a range of other secondary re-inforcers as a result of their good behaviour, such as improved school performance, better relationships at home, more teacher approval, more prestige. It is these other secondary reinforcers that prevented the desired behaviour from collapsing once the experiment was over.

Tharp and Wetzel's experiment is really an example, in the normal school setting, of the *token economy* which behaviour modifiers employ in many closed communities such as approved schools, institutions and hospitals, and in which desired behaviour is rewarded with tokens which are exchanged for treats and privileges (e.g. Lovitt 1970). It also indicates to us that rewards must be things that children genuinely desire, and demonstrates that while children are gaining these rewards they are also acquiring more long term secondary reinforcers that will sustain their improved behaviour in the future.

Criticism of the Learning Theory Approach   A whole literature, for and against, has grown up around Skinner's work (e.g. Wheeler 1973), and in the short space available here we cannot hope to review it. All we shall try to do is to suggest ways of resolving some of the main areas of disagreement between Skinner and the theorists we have been looking at in previous chapters.

The least controversial part of Skinner's argument, and one that is acceptable to most psychologists, is that we often unwittingly re-inforce the very behaviour in children that we wish to discourage. Behaviour modification techniques provide a very useful way of identifying when this is happening, and of doing something to put it right. It is generally accepted that these techniques work best when they are practised throughout the whole of an institution, which means that if they are tried in a school all the staff should be involved in them, and should work out together a common and consistent programme.

Where Skinner is on more controversial ground is in maintaining that behaviour modification techniques can correct all personality problems. His opponents argue that these techniques tackle the symptoms and not the causes of personality malfunction, and that, in the long run, new sets of symptoms are likely to occur in their place. His supporters deny that *symptom substitution* of this kind does happen, as long as all the relevant symptoms in a given category of behaviour problems are tackled in the first place. But of course it is often impossible to do this. In a highly anxious person for example, particularly one with free floating anxiety (chapter 3), anxiety is a generalised reaction to pretty well every aspect of his life.

Another point of criticism in Skinner's work is that much of it (though admittedly by no means all) has been carried out with animals, and it is doubtful how far the results of this work can usefully be applied to humans. Because, for example, we can make an animal behave neurotically, this in no sense demonstrates that anxiety cannot be caused in man through the existence of such a thing as a super-ego. The super-ego is a collection of ideas, values, and beliefs acquired and sustained largely through the use of language. Language gives man a much wider and more complex range of experiences than have animals, and allows him to brood on these experiences, to plan future behaviour, to suffer guilt.

Through the thought processes to which it gives rise, language also helps man to be *aware of the fact that he is being re-inforced.* If he needs the re-inforcement, he produces the appropriate behaviour to obtain it, if not, he withholds the behaviour.

Skinner, of course, denies that man can choose whether to produce behaviour or to withhold it, since this would imply that man has free will, a point that Skinner is not prepared to concede. Here, inevitably, Skinner is straying into a field beset with all kinds of philosophical hazards where 'proof' is not possible one way or another. Indeed it is surprising that Skinner, who prides himself on being a scientist, should allow himself to become involved in a debate of this kind, or to make the kind of categorical statements concerning it that appear so frequently in his work.

From our point of view, and surely from the point of view of any rational person, the important thing is that man thinks and acts *as if* he has free will. Even Skinner, by exhorting mankind to adopt his operant conditioning techniques as the only way to make the world safe for future generations (1972), is behaving *as if* man has the freedom to choose whether to accept his advice or not.

Finally, Skinner's rejection of the notion that man's behaviour can ever be traced to such things as meta needs, raises great problems in the explanation of human motivation. It is not easy to see how a simple operant conditioning model can ever be stretched to explain satisfactorily the work of a Beethoven or a Shakespeare, still less, perhaps, the pleasure that this work has brought to the rest of mankind.

7

Personality and cognition

Personality and Intelligence To speak of personality *and* intelligence is somewhat misleading, since it suggests that the two are quite separate categories of human psychology. If we accept one of the currently popular operational definitions of intelligence — e.g. that it is the ability to overcome difficulties in new situations — we realise that it is very much a part of that general reaction to life that we call personality. When we speak of children as bright, or alert, or dull, it is usually this general reaction that we're talking about, not just the fact that they do well or badly in tests of intelligence. The point is well taken by Cattell, who includes intelligence as one of the factors measured by his personality tests (chapter 5), and by Kelly (chapter 4).

Perhaps what we should be talking about is the relationship between intelligence and other factors of personality therefore. Certainly, intelligence seems to influence some areas of personality more strongly than others. Often there does not seem to be any straightforward link between intelligence and a person's beliefs and values (though it will normally affect the manner in which he can defend them). On the other hand, there will be an obvious connection between intelligence and the level of the goals which a person sets himself in life, and between intelligence and the kind of interpretations that he puts upon his life experiences.

Not surprisingly, since intelligence tests are themselves nomothetic devices, most of the research into the relationship between intelligence and other factors of personality has been carried out by nomothetic rather than by idiographic personality theorists. With the exception of the correlations between low intelligence and 'N' scores mentioned in chapter five, neither Eysenck nor Cattell have found, however, that intelligence correlates *consistently* with any of the dimensions or factors of personality measured in their tests (though we saw, again in chapter 5, some correlation between low intelligence and high 'L' scores).

One very interesting line of research is that carried out by the Fels Institute in the USA into samples of children who, between the ages of six and ten, showed either a marked increase or a marked decline in I.Q. scores (Kagan et al. 1958). It was found that boys were twice as likely as were girls to be in the group that had shown an increase, while there were more girls than boys in the group that had declined (this may be an indication that boys tend to mature later in measured intelligence than do girls, just as they mature later in speech and in reading skills. Alternatively it may be a cultural thing, with boys receiving more challenge and encouragement once they reach school age than do girls). Children in the increased I.Q. group, both boys and girls, were more independent, more competitive, and more verbally aggressive than were those in the declined I.Q. group. They were also readier to work hard, showed a stronger desire to master intellectual problems, and were less likely to withdraw in the face of challenge (this compares interestingly with Coopersmith's findings on high self-esteem boys, chapter 2).

What this research seems to show is that the possession of certain personality characteristics helps children to make full use of their intellectual potential. If we think back to chapter 2, it will be remembered that in higher education as well, Barron found that resourcefulness, energy, and adaptability correlated well with satisfactory levels of achievement. In one of the most ambitious studies of its kind ever attempted, Terman and Oden (1947) followed up 750 children with I.Q.s of 140 plus into adult life, and found that those who fulfilled their early potential were more interested in their work, more persevering, more self-confident, and better integrated in their life goals. They were also significantly better adjusted and more socially effective than the normal population.

Using the terms which we have used in this book so far, we could say that they were higher in achievement motivation, higher in self-esteem, and better adjusted than the average. All these things, of course, correlate strongly with a secure home background, in which the child enjoys the confidence of his parents, and in which he is set definite and consistent standards and encouraged to reach them. However, as Roe (1953) shows, many eminent scientists have struggled against early feelings of inferiority, and the same is true of many great men, so an unfavourable background by no means *ensures* that a person will make little of his life. Adler (chapter 3) would say that such people are struggling extra hard to compensate for this inferiority. Whether his background be favourable or unfavourable though, the person who achieves eminence usually seems to be driven by the need to come up to certain expectations, whether they be formed for him by sympathetic but demanding parents, or by the need to prove his worth in the face of indifference or rejection.

More generally, McCandless (1969) suggests research shows that children with high I.Q.s tend to be taller, handsomer, physically stronger and more popular than those at the opposite end of the spectrum. They also, as pointed out in chapter 5, tend to be less anxious, partly no doubt because they find life easier to manage than do less able children. They also seem better judges of other people (particularly strangers) as well as of themselves, than do less fortunately endowed children. Obviously these high I.Q. children will find in the main that people react favourably to them. They will gain a positive opinion of themselves because others have a positive opinion of them. Thus, in the interaction between heredity and environment, the latter will serve to enhance the former, just as the former will help the child more efficiently to come to terms with the latter. Sadly, the less able child will find himself likely to be handicapped by his environment, by people's low expectations of him, by his failure to achieve competence and eventually, of course, by the low opinion of himself that he develops in the face of the low opinion that others have of him.

Personality and Creativity   This is not the place to enter into a discussion of the nature of creativity. Suffice it to say that psychological research into creativity is of more recent origin than that into intelligence, and that psychologists *suggest* that the latter is characterised by the ability to think *convergently* (i.e. to home in on the unique answer to a problem), and the former by the ability to think *divergently*, that is to come up with as many solutions as possible to a problem that does not necessarily have a unique answer. Because of the absence of a single right answer, tests to measure creativity are known as '*open-ended*' tests, and good examples are the 'Uses of Objects' test (e.g. 'how many uses can you think of for a brick?'), the 'Meanings of Words' test (e.g. 'how many different meanings can you think of for the word "bolt"?'), and visual tests such as converting as many outline drawings of circles as possible into recognisable objects by simply adding details (see e.g. Hudson 1966).

It is still not clear whether intelligence tests and divergent thinking tests are measuring different, related, or the same human attributes. This is partly because the latter tests are still in a relatively crude, experimental form. However, it does seem clear that a certain level of intelligence is needed if an individual is to be able to organise and use his creative talent effectively. It also seems reasonably clear that there is a relationship between high scores on divergent thinking tests and the possession of certain personality characteristics. In a number of studies using the 16 PF, it has been shown that creative people in both the sciences and the arts are more independent, more intellectually self-sufficient, less stable, and more radical than the average (e.g. Cattell and Butcher 1968). Scientists tend to score highly on withdrawal behaviour items, while artists (particularly painters) score on unconventionality and eccentricity (the 'artistic temperament' perhaps). Taylor and Holland (1964) add to this list by suggesting that available evidence shows creative people are more autonomous, self-sufficient, self-assertive, and resourceful. They are also more introverted, more inclined towards feminine interests, more aware of their impulses, and more open to the irrational in themselves. At the risk of lengthening this list too far, we can add that other investigators have found creative people to have a high tolerance of ambiguity (they enjoy puzzling over things that have many possible solutions), and to be capable of a high level of abstract thought. As with intelligence, most studies indicate that people who make effective use of their high levels of creativity are generally strong on achievement motivation. They have a single minded-ness which enables them to work hard in their chosen field and to show a high level of interest and involvement in the things that they do (cf. our comments on the mature personality in chapter 2).

We must stress, however, as we did with intelligence, that creativity should not be seen as something distinct and separate from personality. The creative person is creative in his whole approach to life. Many of the personality characteristics that we mentioned above are not just things that the creative person happens to have, they *are* his creativity as it reveals itself in the business of everyday living. When it comes, therefore, to discussing how best the teacher can encourage creativity in children, much of what we have said already in this book about the teacher's role in helping the child towards maturity and self-actualisation of personality will still apply. Rogers stresses that positive regard and empathic understanding are, as with other areas of personality, the most important contribution the teacher can make towards fostering creativity in children, and to these he adds a *freedom from external evaluation.* This means that although the teacher is free to *react* to children's creative work (i.e. to say whether he likes it or not), he should refrain from passing categorical judgements upon it (i.e. saying it is 'wrong' or 'bad'), since by its very nature divergent activity contains no immutable rules of correctness.

The important part that the teacher can play in allowing the child sufficient freedom to develop his creative powers (Jung, chapter 3, would say in freeing the child to listen to his own unconscious) is evidenced by a number of studies (e.g. Haddon and Lytton 1968) which show that children in informal primary schools perform better on divergent thinking tests than do children in formal schools, and that this enhanced performance persists when the children transfer to secondary schools, irrespective of the type of secondary school involved (Haddon and Lytton 1971). What we are really saying is that if the teacher wishes to encourage the creative side of a child's personality, the child must not be taught to reject this side of himself, and to adopt only a conventional approach to thinking. Hudson (1966) found a tendency amongst boys specialising in science subjects at sixth form level to think convergently, while those specialising in the arts tended to think divergently, and this could well be evidence that some teachers of science subjects are not prepared to allow as much self-expression in their pupils as are some teachers of arts subjects. (Mistakenly, we might add, as there is just as much need to think creatively about science as about the arts.) It seems that when children who are highly convergent are encouraged to be freer and less judgemental in their responses, their ability to think divergently increases markedly.

Jerome Bruner and his colleagues, in a number of studies (e.g. 1956), speak of *holistic* (creative) thinking and *algorithmic* (rational) thinking, and consider that our western educational system encourages the latter at the expense of the former. We lay stress upon conformity, upon children always arriving at the same conclusions as the teacher, upon children always using the 'right' method for solving problems in mathematics and science, upon children not guessing solutions (frequently *guessing*, Bruner argues, is evidence of creative effort, or a sudden flash of insight), upon children not tolerating ambiguity. It is not that Bruner, or indeed any psychologist, argues against the need for convergent, algorithmic thinking, but simply that this kind of thinking should not be the only form of thought encouraged in children. McKellar (1957) puts the case well when he talks of holistic (or, as he chooses to call it, 'autistic') thinking as being the *author* of any worthwhile creative act, while rational thinking is the *editor* who sifts through the ideas generated by holistic thinking, isolates those which are most relevant, and puts them to use.

There is evidence that teachers sometimes find it harder to relate to children high on creativity than to other children. Getzels and Jackson (1962) certainly found this to be the case in their, admittedly rather narrow, sample of teachers and children. They suggest that the creative child's non-conformity and apparent self-sufficiency can make him less immediately sympathetic to teachers than are children with more conformist attributes.

If Getzels and Jackson are right, this means that teachers may sometimes have to take particular care not to allow the creative child's independent outlook to count against him. But this probably applies to all gifted children, whether their giftedness lies in very high creativity, very high intelligence, or both. It is probably another of the failings of our national educational system that we pay insufficient attention to helping the gifted child to live with, and to make good use of, his gifts. Sometimes, though probably not as often as writers in the national press have taken to claiming, the highly gifted child can feel as isolated from other children as can the child of correspondingly low ability. He can also feel as misunderstood and unappreciated. With his high level of curiosity and activity, and his boredom in the face of unchallenging work, he can be a generally uncomfortable member of the class, and some teachers, not surprisingly, feel threatened by his precocious knowledge, and are convinced that he is setting out to score off them in front of the class.

Perhaps because of their very feeling of separateness, there is some evidence that gifted children (particularly, it seems, gifted girls) play down their gifts to avoid antagonising the teacher, and to avoid unpopularity with the rest of the class. Such self-rejection may be potentially as damaging to the personality as are the other forms of self-rejection that we looked at in chapters 3 and 4. The cost to the nation in terms of lost potential needs no emphasising.

Cognitive Style   Cognitive style theorists start from the accepted fact that we are bombarded by so much data from the environment every moment of our lives that we cannot possibly attend to them all without enormous cognitive strain. They then ask *how* do we sort these data out and decide what to attend to and what not, and suggest that we do it by *coding* them, that is by placing each of them into one of a range of categories which carries its own rating of importance. In any situation, things belonging to categories relatively high in importance gain our attention, those belonging to categories relatively low do not.

The way in which we assign things to categories will be partly determined by previous experience, and partly by innate factors, including how we actually *perceive* things (e.g. some people are innately more sensitive to certain stimuli, such as loud noises, bright colours, subtle differences in shape, than are others). We can get a good example of coding from a child tackling a problem. First he studies and categorises the information it contains. Next he hunts through the information in his head until he finds data coded into a similar category. Finally, he forms an hypothesis and sees if it will solve the problem.

Cognitive style theorists claim that we carry out this coding process in our own characteristic and consistent way. We don't change our method drastically from problem to problem. Since our whole contact with the outside world, including our social behaviour, is influenced by the way in which we code, it must be seen as a part, and an important part, of our personalities.

Cognitive style theory is not, however, an alternative to the theories of personality that we have been looking at in the last three chapters. It does not concern itself with motivation, or with the possible systems within the personality, such as the ego and the super-ego, which help to determine why people differ in the degrees of importance which they attach to various categories. For the most part, it seems content to accept that neurotic people may put things into categories which have to do with their worries, and then attend to those which they find the most threatening. It accepts that the extravert may tend to code in terms of his preferences as an extravert, and the introvert in terms of his preferences as an introvert. It accepts that coded categories may become built into personal constructs and so on. It is not so much a theory of personality, as an attempt to explain the actual mechanisms that the personality uses to interact with the world. It is concerned with the way in which we think, and not with why we think in this way or with the content of our thoughts.

We can illustrate this by going back to our example of a child tackling a problem at school. One child may characteristically read quickly through the problem, get an overall, and perhaps inaccurate, picture of what it is all about, and immediately start trying to solve it. Another might characteristically read it through slowly, word by word, before starting work. These different methods of tackling the problem are part and parcel of the children's respective cognitive styles. However, such things as the level of enthusiasm which they bring to bear upon the task, the degrees of importance which they assign to the respective categories which it contains, and the amount of anxiety which they feel if they get it wrong, belong not to their cognitive styles but to those areas of their personality and of their learning discussed in the last three chapters.

Obviously, from an educational point of view, cognitive style is an important aspect of personality. We often find ourselves saying that one child tends to rush things, that another always seems to miss the essentials in an argument, that another is disorganised in his thinking, that another is precise and methodical, and so on. The characteristics represented by those labels are evidenced not only in the way in which children solve problems, but also in the way in which they relate to other people, and in such things as the amount and depth of consideration which they give to their selection of short term and long term life goals.

However, terms such as 'disorganised', 'inconsistent', 'methodical', are somewhat vague and subjective, and various attempts have been made by psychologists to see if there are any more precise — albeit broad — categories of cognitive style into which people can be divided. The results of this research have proved to be rather similar to those produced by the nomothetic approach to personality theory detailed in chapter 5, in that they have tended to identify bi-polar dimensions. These dimensions are still very much in the experimental stage, and the tests upon which they depend are still crude. It is not clear, either, to what extent or in what way they relate to each other, or to personality theories. Nevertheless, three of them are of sufficient interest to be looked at closely, namely *field dependence–independence, focussing–scanning* and *reflectivity–impulsivity.*

Field Dependence–Independence. In one way it is a little unfair to talk of the dimension of field dependence–independence as being still in the experimental stage, since it has been the subject of a formidable amount of research over the last fifteen years, chiefly by the American psychologist Herman Witkin and his colleagues. The impetus for Witkin's work came from the discovery by the United States Air Force that many pilots, on losing visual contact with the ground (as e.g. when they flew into a dense cloud bank), lost all sense of the vertical, and, if unaided by instruments, would often end up unwittingly flying upside down (with consequent increase in combat vulnerability!).

Witkin attempted to study this phenomenon experimentally by constructing the Body Adjustment Test, in which subjects were seated in a tilting chair facing into a small box-like 'room' which could also be tilted (Witkin 1959). When taking the test, some subjects proved able unerringly to say whether they were upright or not irrespective of the angle of the chair and of the 'room', while others lost their sense of the vertical completely as soon as the 'room' in front of them started to tilt; some of them even claimed to be upright when room and chair were both tilting through an angle of thirty degrees. What seemed to be happening was that the first group of subjects was able to sort out the pull of gravity (the relevant stimulus) from the visual experience of the 'room' in front of them (the irrelevant stimulus), whilst the second group was not. Witkin termed the first group field independent (f.i.), and the second group field dependent (f.d.).

Further experiments, using both the embedded figures test, in which the subject first studies a simple black and white line pattern and then has to pick it out when it is 'hidden' in a more complex pattern, and the rod and frame test, in which the subject sits in a darkened room and attempts to place in the vertical a luminous rod which is surrounded by a tilted luminous frame, confirmed the existence of field dependence and field independence as two extremes of a dimension, with the majority of the population, as in the dimensions discussed in chapter 5, located somewhere in the middle.

Witkin then established that this dimension has interesting applications in everyday life. For example, f.d. people seem less able to pick out and remember the details in a given situation that can f.i. When presented with a battery of projective techniques (chapter 3), they also disclose themselves as less perceptive in dealing with life, and more easily influenced (Witkin et al. 1954). Witkin sums this up by saying that the f.d. person has a *global* cognitive style, while the f.i. has an *articulated* one (these terms, global and articulated, together with the group label *psychological differentiation*, are tending to replace field dependence–independence).

Since correlations have been found between extraversion and field dependence (Witkin 1959), it is tempting to suggest that the latter is to some extent an expression of the former. The extravert, with his greater social involvement, his greater need for frequent and varied stimuli, and his slower rate of conditioning, pays less attention to each unit of experience, is more readily swayed by group opinion, and gives himself less time to be perceptive about which are the most relevant units of experience in any given situation. He is therefore logically somewhat more likely to be f.d. than is the introvert.

However, it would be wrong to regard the dimension of field dependence–independence as lying precisely along the same dimension as extraversion–introversion. Though there is a correlation, it is far from being a perfect one. Many extraverts are f.i., just as many introverts are f.d. For field independence also seems to go with certain things that extraverts possess as frequently as do introverts, such as a more developed sense of personal identity (which in Erikson's terms, remember, indicates maturity of personality — chapter 2), and with higher self-esteem and self-confidence. Interestingly, it also goes with a particular style of ego defence mechanism (chapter 3). Bertini (1961) demonstrates that when f.i. people employ repression, they seem able to repress selectively, whereas f.d. people are likely to repress indiscriminately, blotting out large chunks of their past experience in a way which suggests they are much less able, consciously or unconsciously, to single out the precise causes of their anxiety. F.d. people are also better able than are f.i. to keep their feelings separate from their thoughts and perceptions, which could be one of the reasons why field dependence correlates more strongly with women than with men.

It is important to stress that although much of what we have been saying seems to favour field independence over dependence, Witkin is at pains to point out that, as with something like extraversion–introversion, neither is 'better' than the other. The f.d. person might be more sensitive to the needs of others than is the f.i., more gregarious, more socially involved, perhaps less likely to withdraw. *Extremes* at either end of the dimensions are equally adverse, with the f.d. person tending to suffer from identity defusion and over dependence upon others (alcoholics and compulsive over-eaters are often field dependent), and the f.i. person from a too rigid defence of personal identity which leads him to lay the blame for his problems always upon others rather than to blame (and try to change) himself.

Field dependence–independence has obvious implications for the teacher in terms of children's inter-personal relationships and their approach to problem solving. Although it throws little light on creativity (different kinds of creativity may possibly demand different kinds of style), it does have bearing upon intelligence. Studies show that f.i. children perform better on analytical items in I.Q. tests than do f.d., though there is no difference on verbal items. Witkin (1965) argues that as many ESN children also score more highly on analytical items than they do on verbal, and that as many children with low analytical scores are often not diagnosed as ESN because this poor performance is disguised by high verbal ability, I.Q. tests should be replaced by those for cognitive style, since the latter are more comprehensive and 'recognise the rooting of intellectual functioning in personality'.

Focussing–Scanning is associated particularly with the American psychologist Jerome Bruner, now at the University of Oxford. Unlike Witkin, the main impetus behind Bruner's work comes from research with children. Again unlike Witkin, this research has concentrated upon observing the coding systems (called by Bruner *strategies*) which are adopted in a problem solving situation. One of Bruner's best known tests is to present the child with a number of pairs of cards, one pair at a time, each card consisting of varying arrangements of squares, circles, lines and colours. The child is then told that one card in each pair is 'correct' and the other 'incorrect', and as more of the pairs are presented to him, he is asked to determine what particular features of the squares, circles, etc., denotes 'correctness' and 'incorrectness' (Bruner et al. 1956).

Research of this kind appears to indicate that children are distributed along a dimension, at one end of which are those who examine the relevant features in each of the pairs until they have amassed enough information to advance an hypothesis (the *focussers*), and at the other end are those who form an hypothesis on the basis of the first pair, stick to it until eventually enough subsequent pairs have been examined to show it to be untenable, and then have to go back to the beginning and start again (the *scanners*).

What seems to be happening is that focussers characteristically delay hypothesis-making until they have enough evidence, while scanners characteristically form an hypothesis on slimmer evidence, and have no option but to begin afresh if subsequently they are shown to be wrong. If the same strategies are applied in social situations, we might say that the focusser makes up his mind about other people only when he has got to know them well, whereas the scanner makes up his mind more quickly, sometimes only to have to abandon this opinion altogether (and along with it, perhaps, a friendship), when the evidence against it becomes too strong.

The importance to teachers of the focussing–scanning dimension is considerable. Children who scan, it seems, have a particular need to be allowed to go back and check earlier clues if their original hypothesis becomes untenable, and therefore may be at a disadvantage in mentally presented problems. Children who focus, on the other hand, may delay too long over forming their hypotheses, and thus be handicapped in work involving quick responses. On the teacher's own part, there is the risk that the scanner may make snap decisions on children, and then have to recant later (e.g. with such remarks in a school report as 'has deteriorated this term, must do better next', which may confuse the child as much as it worries his parents), while the focusser may be over-cautious in giving praise, or good marks, or in writing an enthusiastic report or reference.

Ideally, people should be able to focus or to scan, depending upon the nature of the problem they are called upon to tackle, the amount of time in which they have to do it, and so on. Sometimes a quick hypothesis is called for, sometimes a more cautious one. Extreme focussing can be a sign of insecurity (if you never reach a decision about anything, you can never be proved wrong), and may lead to sitting on the fence until the opportunity has been lost (e.g. someone else proposes to the girl). Extreme scanning on the other hand can mean an early commitment with little hope of retrieving the situation later (the wedding bells sound too early). When solving each problem, one should be a good judge of how long one can delay one's decision while awaiting further evidence.

Again there are no clear correlations between focussing–scanning and creativity (or between it and intelligence). Probably extremes of either are less helpful than a judicious combination of the two. There is also little link between Bruner's dimension and Witkin's (scanners are not, as one might suppose, f.d. and focussers f.i.), though it is not unreasonable to hope that future research, with more sophisticated measuring devices, may reveal a relationship of some kind between them.

Reflectivity–Impulsivity. The third dimension that we are to examine is proposed by another American psychologist, Jerome Kagan. If we think back to the beginning of this section, it will be remembered that there are typically three stages in problem solving, firstly categorising the given information, secondly sifting mentally through one's own knowledge to find similar categories, and thirdly forming an hypothesis with which to proceed to the solution. Kagan considers that cognitive style particularly influences the first and last of those stages. Some people, he claims (1966), characteristically act *reflectively* in categorising the information and producing their hypotheses, whilst others behave *impulsively.*

Kagan also claims to have discovered another dimension, *visual analysis,* which relates to the extent to which people break down the information in stage one. Some people, at least with a visually presented problem, tend to break it down into small units, whilst others prefer to work with much larger chunks of it. Perhaps oddly, there is no strong correlation between visual analysis and reflectivity–impulsivity. Some reflective people work with large chunks of information and some with small, and the same is true of impulsive people.

Kagan has devised a number of tests to explore these two dimensions. In the Delayed Recall of Design Test, which is a test of reflectivity–impulsivity, the child is presented with a simple black and white design for a few seconds, and is then asked to pick it out from a number of similar designs. The test is scored for response time and for accuracy, and typically, reflective children take longer over their responses and make fewer errors than do impulsive children. In the Visual Analysis Test, the child learns to associate respectively four nonsense syllables with four complex designs, each containing several components, and is then asked to produce the correct syllable when he is shown only single components abstracted from each design. The visually analytic child, who has had no difficulty in analysing each design into its separate components, makes far fewer mistakes than does the unanalytic child, to whom each of the designs exists only as a complete unit.

As with Witkin and Bruner, Kagan's work has important potential implications for education. At present, most of these implications must be drawn from the reflectivity–impulsivity dimension, as the visual analysis dimension is still very much in the experimental stage. Leaving aside a small group of highly anxious children who have a long response time and still make many errors, it seems clear that on challenging and difficult problems at least, reflective children make significantly fewer errors than do impulsive ones. Kagan (1966) claims that they show a strong desire to be right first time, and seem able to tolerate the ambiguity of a long silence (not easy if perhaps both teacher and class are waiting impatiently to see if they know the answer or not) while they weigh each possibility before responding. Impulsive children, on the other hand, adopt a 'shotgun' approach, firing out several answers, either in the hope that one will prove correct or because they rely upon feedback from the teacher rather than upon their own internal reflections to tell them if they are getting 'warm' or not. Kagan says that reflective children have a slow, and impulsive children a fast, *conceptual tempo*.

Conceptual tempo also seems important in serial learning tasks. For example, when learning vocabulary lists, impulsive children tend to make more errors of commission (i.e. including extra words in the recalled list) than do reflective children, and the more critical the teacher becomes, the more of these errors they make. When reading, they tend to make more orthographic errors, typically by misreading simple three letter words (e.g. 'log' for 'dog', 'cat' for 'pat'), even when they are perfectly familiar with the individual letters concerned.

Like Witkin and Bruner, Kagan resists the conclusion that it is necessarily 'better' to be reflective than impulsive, though the former does seem associated with maturity in that as children grow older their reflectivity scores tend to increase (though the *relative* differences between impulsive and reflective children may remain the same). He suggests that whereas high reflectivity may be advantageous in academic subjects like maths, it may be a disadvantage in the visual arts and in some aspects of the humanities and social sciences. However, Kagan does concede that the highly impulsive child's frequent experience of selecting the wrong hypothesis may be a source of discouragement, and lead to increased anxiety and greater impulsivity as he tries to put things right.

Further Research into Cognitive Style. It is by no means clear whether it is possible to change a child's cognitive style on any of the dimensions mentioned. Relative positions on each of them seem to remain markedly stable over the years and Kagan concludes that cognitive style may be a 'basic component of the individual's behavioural organisation' (1966). More research is needed before the point is proved, and hopefully such research will also show whether tests of cognitive style are the improvement on tests of intelligence that Witkin claims them to be, and whether they can be usefully used by teachers when deciding how best to structure the learning situation to suit individual children.

We also need to know more about the relationship between the various dimensions of cognitive style so far discovered, more about their relationship to intelligence and creativity, and much more about their relationship to the causal factors in personality development. As we have seen, a start has been made in relating cognitive style to ego defence mechanisms, to personal identity, and to particular forms of personality problems. But what part does an individual's sense of security, of confidence, of self-esteem, etc. have to play in his style? And is style more a product of, or a cause of, these things? And how does cognitive style affect the way in which one forms one's personal constructs, or the freedom with which one locomotes through one's life space, or the methods which one employs to deal with cognitive dissonance? The subject is rich in research possibilities.

8

Mental ill-health

When discussing Freud's contribution to psychology in chapter 3, we said that he has given us the notion that normal and abnormal behaviour are simply different points on the same continuum. To some degree we all have personality problems, and decisions on when these problems are bad enough to be classified as mental ill health are largely cultural ones. Such decisions differ from society to society, from generation to generation, and from individual to individual.

Much of what we can say about mental ill-health we have therefore been saying throughout the book, and the purpose of the present chapter is more to discuss definitions than to go back over ground already covered. This is particularly true of maladjustment, which we shall look at first.

Maladjustment We have deliberately avoided the term maladjustment throughout the book, but in a sense, this is really what we have been talking about every time we have made any mention of the problems that can occur in the developing personality. The term maladjustment is often taken to mean the behaviour of particularly unruly, violent, and disruptive children, which is why we have steered clear of the term, but in its correct sense it means all children who are experiencing special problems in relating to others and to themselves. The Underwood Report (1955), which is still the principal official statement in this country on the subject, defines the maladjusted child as 'one who is developing in ways that have a bad effect on

155

himself or his fellows, and cannot without help be remedied by his parents, teachers, and other adults in normal contact with him'.

Though this definition begs such questions as what is meant by 'a bad effect', it is a useful one in that it obviously includes within the scope of maladjustment the withdrawn and isolated child as well as the gang leader, the nervous and highly strung child as well as the violent one, the child who cannot communicate as well as the one who communicates too loudly and selfishly.

We have said enough about these problems in the book to show that psychologists are generally agreed that the causes lie very much in faulty relationships between the child and his parents or substitute parents, particularly during the critical first five or six years of his life, but essentially throughout the whole of his childhood and adolescence. Low self-esteem, high levels of guilt, reinforcement incorrectly applied, constant demands for inappropriate behaviour, the absence of love and of emotional security, the absence of sympathy and understanding — all these things go to make the maladjusted child. Psychologists may disagree about the actual mechanisms involved, but they all accept that maladjustment is a cry for help from a child who is largely the victim of the inadequacies of his elders. The child who is forced to live with inconsistency or with fear and with a sense of rejection, the child who is forced to live with conflict between the various areas of his life or who is constantly reminded of his own inadequacies, is hardly likely to learn to relate to the world around him in a positive and satisfying way.

We have also said enough about these problems to show that their cure lies in reversing the processes that have caused them. Acceptance in the place of rejection, concern in the place of uninterest, sympathy in the place of indifference, consistency in the place of inconsistency, encouragement in the place of censure, harmony in the place of conflict. But there remains one point that we still have to stress. The class teacher, with his class of thirty children and all the numerous demands that are made of him, cannot hope to set the world to rights on his own. Even if he did have more time to spend with the individual victims of maladjustment, he shares only a part of a child's life. The child belongs to the world outside school as well as to the world inside. He belongs to the home and the peer group, to the values of his local community, and although the teacher may be able to do a great deal to help him, he cannot be expected to do it all.

This is why, to return to the Underwood Report's definition of maladjustment, we must emphasise that it says the problem of the maladjusted child 'cannot be remedied by his parents, teachers, and other adults in normal contact with him'. The maladjusted child, in other words, needs specialist help. So part of the teacher's job with such children is therefore a diagnostic one. He should be able to identify anyone in his class who may be maladjusted, and then refer him, through the headteacher, for assessment and possibly for treatment by the child guidance service. Having done so, he must try to see that the referral is carried out.

Hyperactivity Hyperactivity is a personality disorder that is often dealt with under maladjustment, but it merits a separate section since it is not clear that it really stems from the same causes. Hyperactivity, as the name suggests, is constant and extreme restlessness. In studying a group of hyperactive children between the ages of five and eleven, Stewart (1970) found this restlessness included inability to finish work, talkativeness, clumsiness, unpredictability, inability to stick at games, and a general resistance to discipline. Not surprisingly, the children's school work was well below average.

Hyperactive behaviour seems to manifest itself as early as the first year of life, and to persist through into adolescence. One commonly accepted theory is that it is due to brain damage, but Stewart found no evidence for this in his sample. Nor was there any obvious causal factor in the environment, as there typically is in maladjustment (though some maladjusted children do exhibit hyperactivity amongst their other symptoms). Stewart suggests the cause may be some chromosomal abnormality, and it is known that the condition can be medically controlled with amphetamines, which act indirectly upon the hypothalamus (one of the areas of the brain that, as we saw in chapter 5, may be involved in some way in personality). Marston and Scott (1970), who call the condition 'Inconsequentiality' (or 'Q'), and suggest it is related to high impulsivity scores on Kagan's reflectivity-impulsivity dimension, also consider it may be congenital in origin because hyperactive children are generally poor scorers on such tests of innate ability as motor performance.

The hyperactive child can be a great strain on the teacher's patience. In addition to the characteristics mentioned by Stewart, it was found by Marston and Scott that hyperactive children are often insolent, untidy, slapdash, and given to clowning and showing off. Something like four per cent of children may fall into this category, with boys outnumbering girls by six to one. The teacher should remember that the hyperactive child may have little conscious control over his behaviour. There is no point in insisting that he keep still, and it may be that it is the very frustrations and checkings that he receives from adults which lead to his insolence and clowning, and to the low self-esteem which he shows as an adolescent (Stewart 1970). It may even be that it is these that sometimes cause the maladjustment in those instances where maladjustment and hyperactivity go together.

Ideally, the hyperactive child should be given scope by the teacher for his constant need for activity. A long attention span should not be demanded of him, and of course he should never be labelled as meddlesome, or as a nuisance; nor should he be made to feel odd in any way. As such children are usually extraverted, they should never be denied group work whatever problems this may bring, and they sometimes, in fact, respond well to the opportunities of group leadership. They are often of above average intelligence (McCandless 1969), and there is some evidence that behaviour modification techniques (chapter 5), which involve praising them for periods of concentration and co-operation, and for the initiative and inventiveness which they often show, are of value in helping them learn self-control.

Psychopathy (or Sociopathy) Psychopathy is an extreme form of personality disorder, often correlated with delinquent and anti-social activity. Fundamentally, the psychopath is a person who cannot experience the emotions normally present in inter-personal behaviour. He seems unable to feel affection, sympathy or remorse. He is selfish, superficial, and indifferent both to the feelings of others and to fear or punishment. He demands instant gratification for his own impulses, regardless of the long-term consequences to himself or to other people. He has a pathological disregard for the truth, and can be distinguished from other neurotic or emotionally disturbed children by his complete absence of guilt.

Psychoanalysts would argue that the psychopath is someone who has failed to develop a super-ego, and someone in whom even the ego seems insufficiently reality orientated. The reasons for this failure seem to be both physiological and environmental. Summarising research into the former, Hare (1970) suggests that psychopathy may be related to brain immaturity, as even in adult life psychopaths show an excessive amount of the slow brain waves usually found in children. Of more relevance in the light of our discussion of the physiology of extraversion-introversion and neuroticism-stability (chapter 5), the psychopath seems to have a low level of arousal in the autonomic nervous system. Perhaps he therefore needs an excessive amount of stimulation to achieve the 'kicks' that arousal of this system brings. Eysenck, who it will be remembered has devised a test to measure many of the factors associated with psychopathy, suggests that the condition may be linked to a degree of unstable extraversion so extreme that it is way beyond the range measured by the extraversion–introversion dimension.

Environmentally, psychopaths often come from broken and loveless homes, with fathers who are alcoholic or themselves psychopathic. There is some suggestion that the psychopath may be modelling the cold and inconsistent behaviour of his parents, while Arieti (1967) thinks he may be a victim of a complete lack of impulse training and of social control.

However, in view of the early age at which psychopathy typically manifests itself, it is probable that genetic factors outweigh environmental ones in importance.

No reliable evidence exists on the incidence of psychopathy in the population, though it is known that males far outnumber females. Distressingly, there is often little that the teacher can do to help the psychopath. The latter's callous and sadistic behaviour, and his constant betrayal of trust, may outrage the teacher, but since the psychopath seems unable to experience remorse, moral lectures and appeals to his better nature usually have little effect. Psychopaths are generally of normal intelligence, and can learn things unconnected with emotional responses readily enough, which often means they quickly find out how to manipulate others. Thus instead of their usual callous aggressiveness, they may adopt with those who are trying to help them a guise of charming plausibility, or may become parasitic, relying upon apparent helplessness and repeated, insincere promises of remorse and of atonement to get their own way.

Like the teacher, the psychologist has no markedly effective means of rehabilitating the psychopath. Sometimes the latter seems to settle into more reasonable social behaviour in adult life, but in many cases, effective treatment, if it comes, may rely upon psychopharmacology (mood changing drugs), or upon long-stay institutional care, probably with the consistent application of behaviour modification techniques.

Mental illness   There is sometimes confusion in people's minds between mental illness (psychosis) and the extreme forms of the anxiety that we have been referring to throughout the book (neurosis). This is not surprising, as the distinction is by no means a clear one. However, it is generally accepted by psychologists and by psychiatrists that whereas *neurosis* allows the subject to carry on the semblance of a normal life, often with the awareness that he is seriously disturbed and needs help, in *psychosis* he is unable to do so and requires hospitalisation. Typically, the psychotic patient is unaware that he is ill, and seems to have lost contact with reality. Unlike neurotic behaviour, it is possible that psychotic behaviour is not on a continuum with normal behaviour (Maher 1970), though as we shall see shortly, it is possible that it owes its origin to some of the same causes.

It would be inappropriate to spend too long on a description of the psychoses, since these fall within the province of clinical rather than educational psychology, but generally they are categorised into two distinct, though perhaps overlapping, forms, *schizophrenic* and *manic depressive*. A third form, *paranoic*, is possibly a subdivision of the former. In *schizophrenic psychosis* (schizophrenia), which accounts for the largest single group of patients in our mental hospitals, the individual sometimes loses all sense of personal identity. He suffers from auditory and visual hallucinations, he may show deviant motor behaviour (e.g. retaining the same position for long periods), perceptual abnormalities (colours and sounds may become intense, or he may lose his sense of his own body image) and, most strikingly of all, he may show thought disorders which rob him of the ability to communicate logically with others. In the course of these disorders, he may withdraw altogether from human contact, or he may show an incompatibility between the idea which he is trying to express and the emotion that accompanies it — hence the term 'split personality' which is sometimes applied to schizophrenics (e.g. he may talk of sad things with joy and of joyful things with sadness).

In *manic depressive psychosis*, the patient often retains some measure of rapport with others, but his behaviour is characterised by violent mood swings, from extreme elation (mania) to extreme despondency (depression). Sometimes these swings are brought about by environmental factors, but more often they are spontaneous, and any attempt to reason with the patient usually meets with failure. In *paranoia*, the patient may remain more coherent than the schizophrenic, but he shows the same capacity for delusions, except that these are consistently organised into two kinds, delusions of his own importance, and delusions that others are persecuting him.

Little is certain about the causes of mental illness. There is some evidence to link schizophrenia with introversion, and manic depressive psychosis with extraversion (Eysenck 1969), and this suggests there may be a constitutional factor of some kind at work here (a suggestion supported by Sheldon's findings that schizophrenia is more common amongst ectomorphic people and manic depressive psychosis amongst endomorphs — see chapter 1 above). However, the old idea that mental illness is directly inherited is untenable, though people may differ in their resistance to the pressures that bring on this illness.

Extensive but inconclusive research has been carried out into the nature of these pressures, particularly with schizophrenia (see Lowe 1969 for a survey). The consensus seems to be that these pressures begin in early childhood, and are of the same order as those implicated in the neuroses, except that in schizophrenia there may often be present what Bateson and his colleagues (1956) call the *double bind* situation. This situation is a form of inconsistency, particularly within the mother-child relationship, in which the child habitually has certain kinds of behaviour demanded of him and then is criticised for producing them (as for example when the mother tells the child not to pester her with his chatter, and then accuses him of sulking when he tries to be quiet). The double bind punishes the child emotionally whatever he does, and he has no chance to acquire the capacity to distinguish logic in human behaviour. Not surprisingly, he withdraws increasingly from relationships with others. Bannister (1960) suggests that in terms of construct theory (chapter 4), the double bind means that the child's personal constructs are constantly being invalidated. Laing and Esterson (1964) present several case studies illustrating the double bind in action, and also some of the other emotional pressures that the schizophrenic person can come under from his family, in particular from a mother who is often dominating and restrictive, and who consistently interprets her child's behaviour in terms of her own feelings.

The causes of manic depressive psychosis have attracted less attention. Psychoanalysts hold manic depression to be a sign that, through psychological frustrations in the very early years of life, the individual is still fixated in the infantile feeding cycle of hunger ('depression') and satiety ('mania'). Other studies suggest it is linked with a sense of repressed failure, which on occasion overwhelms the individual and from which he attempts to break free.

Perhaps it is a sign of our confusing times that mental illness is on the increase. At some time in our lives, more than one in ten of us will need psychiatric help, women being more vulnerable than men. Ryle (1969) shows that the problem is not an inconsiderable one amongst students in higher education, and schizophrenia, in particular, sometimes manifests its presence as early as the adolescent years. The treatment of mental illness belongs to the consulting room and not to the school, but the teacher should be alert for the symptoms, and prompt to refer the child concerned for specialist help.

Briefly, in schizophrenia these early symptoms often involve increasingly withdrawn behaviour, in which the adolescent or young adult seems unable to relate satisfactorily to others, and may even show sudden and apparently groundless suspicion and hostility towards them. There may be a marked deterioration in his standards of personal appearance, and in his study habits and his general ability to organise his life. Subsequently, these symptoms may become further complicated by irrational and even bizarre thought patterns, and an inability to follow a consecutive or logical argument, or to manifest the kind of emotions that others feel are appropriate.

In manic depressive psychosis, the symptoms may take a rather different, less irrational form, with the individual showing extreme restlessness or uncharacteristic apathy or, disconcertingly, violent and unaccountable fluctuations between the two. Initially, study habits and thought patterns are less likely to suffer than in schizophrenia, and, far from withdrawing, the individual may show increased demands upon the company and support of others. But as with schizophrenia, the need for specialist help becomes increasingly apparent, and the sooner this help is given, the more promising the long-term prognosis.

Conclusion

In some ways it is a pity that we have ended on the theme of mental illness. Psychologists are commonly accused of looking too frequently on the negative side of human personality rather than on the positive. This is partly, of course, because so much of their work has been with people who have problems. Like the medical doctor, the psychologist often tends not to see much of people when they are well. Many of our insights into personality come, therefore, from the clinical work of people like Freud, Rogers, or Kelly. Even a psychologist like Eysenck, who has done so much to establish personality testing with 'normal' people, has spent much of his professional life helping those who are mentally disturbed.

But this being said, I hope we have stressed strongly enough that few psychologists now see the normal and the abnormal personality as two quite separate things. Whether it be Freud talking about normal and abnormal behaviour as being on a continuum, or Eysenck measuring neuroticism by a single dimension somewhere on which we all find our place, psychologists stress that through the study of even the most unfortunate and disturbed of our fellow men we gain insights into what it means, essentially, to be human.

Perhaps we can leave this point by saying that humanistic psychologists in particular, but probably all psychologists in their heart of hearts, see man as characterised by joy as well as by suffering, by hope as well as by despair. The teacher is uniquely placed to see both sides of man, and to see them, moreover, as they develop from the experimental world of childhood to the more formed and self-assured one of late adolescence and early adulthood.

The other thing I hope I have stressed enough is that although psychologists' ideas about personality seem to cover such a disparate range, there is a pattern there, if we look for it. Not always a harmonious pattern, and not always a very finished one, but a pattern nevertheless. Although psychonalysts may argue with behaviourists, and behaviourists with humanists, to the teacher, who is a practical person and has to get on with the business of educating children, there is something there that can be learnt from them all. The trouble with conflict, in any academic discipline, is that it sometimes tends to polarise opinion unnecessarily. People take up opposing positions, and ignore the common ground that exists between them. Psychologists, at times, make too much of their differences, and not enough of their similarities.

Finally, I hope that the picture to emerge from this book of the kind of teacher best able to help children's personality development doesn't seem too daunting a one. But the underlying theme, without which the book becomes meaningless, is that each child, each individual personality, is unique. Children share the same needs, and the same kind of developmental pattern, but the emphasis within each child is different. That is why teaching can be such a difficult task. There are no glib formulas that work for everybody, in every case. Which means, as Rogers and as Kelly would insist, that to relate to children we must learn to understand their individual phenomenal worlds and their individual constructs. Only then can we help them become confident, open, and hopeful adults.

Further reading

Chapter 1
BEADLE, M. (1972) *A Child's Mind* (London: Methuen)
MUSSEN, P. H., CONGER, J., and KAGAN, J. (1974) *Child Development and Personality* (New York: Harper Row)

Chapter 2
ALLPORT, G. W. (1961) *Pattern and Growth in Personality* (New York: Holt, Rinehart and Winston)
DAVIE, R., BUTLER, N., and GOLDSTEIN, H. (1972) *From Birth to Seven* (London: Longmans)
MAYS, J. B. (ed.) (1972) *Juvenile Delinquency, the Family, and the Social Group* (London: Longmans)
McCANDLESS, B. R. (1969) *Children: Behavior and Development* (New York: Holt, Rinehart and Winston)

Chapters 3, 4 and 5
BANNISTER, D. and FRANSELLA, F. (1971) *Inquiring Man: the Theory of Personal Constructs* (Harmondsworth: Penguin)
BROWN, J. A. C. (1964) *Freud and the Post-Freudians* (Harmondsworth: Pelican)
CATTELL, R. B. (1965) *The Scientific Analysis of Personality* (Harmondsworth: Pelican)
EYSENCK, H. J. and EYSENCK, S. (1969) *The Structure and Measurement of Personality* (London: Routledge and Kegan Paul)
HALL, C. S. and LINDZEY, G. (1970) *Theories of Personality* (New York: Wiley) (Also recommended reading for chapter 6)
HOLT, R. (1971) *Assessing Personality* (New York: Harcourt, Brace, Jovanovich) (Also recommended reading for chapter 7)
NAYLOR, F. D. (1972) *Personality and Educational Achievement* (Sydney: Wiley)

WARREN, N. and JAHODA, M. (eds) (1973) *Attitudes* (Harmondsworth: Penguin)
The personality tests that are mentioned in these chapters, where they do not appear separately in the References and Name Index, are either available from the National Foundation for Educational Research or are described in:
ANASTASI, A. (1968) *Psychological Testing* (New York: MacMillan)

Chapter 6
BANDURA, A. (1969) *Principles of Behavior Modification* (New York: Holt, Rinehart and Winston)
BIGGE, L. (1976) *Learning Theories for Teachers* (New York: Harper Row)
CARPENTER, R. (1974) *The Skinner Primer* (New York: Free Press)
POTEET, J. A. (1974) *Behaviour Modification* (London: University of London Press)

Chapter 7
VERNON, P. E. (ed.) (1970) *Creativity* (Harmondsworth: Penguin)
WARR, P. B. (ed.) (1970) *Thought and Personality* (Harmondsworth: Penguin)

Chapter 8
MAHER, B. A. (1970) *Principles of Psychopathology* (New York: McGraw Hill)
WILLIAMS, P. (ed.) (1974) *Behaviour Problems in School* (London: University of London Press)

References and Name index

The numbers in italics following each entry are page
references to discussions of authors within this book.

Note: for references to personality tests that appear in the text, but
are not listed below, see *Further Reading*.

ADLER, A. (1939) *Social Interest* (New York: Putnam). *63-6, 70-2, 95,
140*

ALLPORT, G. W. (1961) *Pattern and Growth in Personality* (London:
Holt, Rinehart and Winston. *12, 43-5, 70, 97, 166*

ANDRY, R. (1960) *Delinquency and Parental Pathology* (London:
Methuen). *40*

ANTONY, W. S. (1973) 'The development of extroversion, of ability,
and of the relation between them', *British Journal of Educational
Psychology* **43**, 3. *107*

ARIETI, S. (1967) *The Intrapsychic Self* (New York: Basic Books). *159*

ASCH, S. E. (1955) 'Opinions and social pressure', *Scientific American*,
November. *91, 115*

BANDURA, A. (1969) *Principles of Behaviour Modification* (New York:
Holt, Rinehart and Winston). *129-31, 134, 167*

BANDURA, A. (1973) *Aggression; a Social Learning Analysis*
(Englewood Cliffs: Prentice-Hall). *130*

BANNISTER, D. (1960) 'Conceptual structure in thought disordered
schizophrenics', *J. ment. Sci.* 106. *162, 166*

BARKER LUNN, J. C. (1969) 'The development of scales to measure
junior school children's attitudes', *British Journal of Educational
Psychology* **39**, 1. *120*

BARRON, F. (1954) 'Personal soundness in university graduate
students'. *Publications in Personality Assessment and Research No. 1*
(Berkeley: University of California Press). *44, 108*

BATESON, G., JACKSON, D., HALEY, J., and WEAKLAND, J. (1956)
'Towards a theory of schizophrenia', *Behavioral Science* **1**. *162*

BENNETT, S. M. (1973) 'A re-evaluation of the JEPI', *British Journal of
Educational Psychology* **43**, 2. *111-12*

BERTINI, M. (1961) 'Il tratto dell'isolamento nella sua determinazione dinamica e strutturale', *Contributi dell' Instituto di Psicologica* **25**. *149*

BRONSON, G. (1962) 'Critical periods in human development', *British Journal of Educational Psychology* **35**, 2. *21*

BROWN, J. A. C. (1964) *Freud and the Post Freudians* (Harmondsworth: Pelican). *50, 63, 166*

BRUNER, J., GOODNOW, J., and AUSTIN, G. (1956) *A Study of Thinking* (New York: Wiley). *143, 150-3*

CALLARD, M. and GOODFELLOW, C. (1962) 'Neuroticism and extroversion in schoolboys as measured by the junior MPI', *Journal of Educational Psychology* **61**. *104*

CATTELL, R. B. (1965) *The Scientific Analysis of Personality* (Harmondsworth: Pelican). *112-13, 121, 138, 139, 166*

CATTELL, R. B. and BUTCHER, H. J. (1968) *The Prediction of Achievement and Creativity* (New York: Bobbs-Merrill). *141*

CATTELL, R. B., DUNCAN, B., and BELOFF, J. (1955) 'The inheritance of personality', *American Journal of Human Genetics* **7**. *8*

CAUDILL, W. and WEINSTEIN, H. (1966) 'Maternal care and infant behaviour in Japanese and American middle class families', in Konig, R. and Hill, R. (eds) *Yearbook of the International Sociological Association.* *19*

CHANAN, G. and DELAMONT, S. (1975) (eds) *Frontiers of Classroom Research* (Slough: NFER). *122*

CHILD, D. (1970) *The Essentials of Factor Analysis* (London: Holt, Rinehart and Winston). *102*

CONGER, J. J. and MILLER, W. C. (1966) *Personality, Social Class, and Delinquency* (New York: Wiley). *40*

COOPERSMITH, S. (1968) 'Studies in self-esteem', *Scientific American* February. *31-6, 40, 96, 139*

CORTIS, G. A. (1973) 'The assessment of a group of teachers in relation to earlier career experience', *Ed. Rev.* **25**, 2. *121, 122*

CRUTCHFIELD, R. S. (1955) Conformity and character. *American Psychologist* **10**. *91*

DAVIE, R., BUTLER, N., and GOLDSTEIN, H. (1972) *From Birth to Seven* (London: Longmans). *27, 34-6, 166*

ELLIOTT, C. D. (1972) 'Personality factors and scholastic attainment', *British Journal of Educational Psychology* **42**, 1. *104*

ENTWISTLE, N. J. (1968) 'Academic motivation and school attainment', *British Journal of Educational Psychology* **38**, 2. *120*

ENTWISTLE, N. J. (1972) 'Personality and academic attainment', *British Journal of Educational Psychology* **42**, 2. *107*

ENTWISTLE, N. J., NISBET, J., ENTWISTLE, D., and COWELL, M. (1971) 'The academic performance of students', *British Journal of Educational Psychology* **41**, 3. *120*

ERIKSON, E. H. (1950) *Childhood and Society* (New York: Norton). *22-46, 50, 70*

ERIKSON, E. H. (1959) 'Growth and crisis in the healthy personality'. *Psychological Issues* **1**. *22*

ESCALONA, S. and HEIDER, G. M. (1959) *Prediction and Outcome: a Study in Child Development* (New York: Basic Books). *12*

EYSENCK, H. J. (1956) 'The inheritance of extraversion–introversion', *Acta Psychology* **12**. *7*

EYSENCK, H. J., ARNOLD, W. J., and MEILI, R. (1975) *Encyclopedia of Psychology Vol. 2* (London: Fontana/Collins). *3*

EYSENCK, H. J. and COOKSON, D. (1969) 'Personality in primary school children', *British Journal of Educational Psychology* **39**, 2. *104*

EYSENCK, H. J. and EYSENCK, S. B. (1969) *Personality Structure and Measurement* (London: Routledge and Kegan Paul). *8, 98-113, 127-8, 139, 159, 162, 164, 166*

EYSENCK, S. B., NIAS, D., and EYSENCK, H. J. (1971) 'The interpretation of children's lie scale scores', *British Journal of Educational Psychology* **41**, 1. *110*

FESTINGER, L. (1962) 'Cognitive dissonance', *Scientific American* October. *117-19*

FREUD, S. (1953-64) *The Complete Psychological Works*, 24 Vols. J. Strachey (ed.) (London: Hogarth). *49-66, 70, 71, 73-7, 82, 99, 111, 115, 123, 132, 155, 164*

FURNEAUX, W. D. (1957) 'The use of psychological tests for the selection of students to the department of aeronautics', *Imperial College Report* (unpublished). *105*

GETZELS, J. W. and JACKSON, P. W. (1962) *Creativity and Intelligence* (New York: Wiley). *144*

GOLDFARB, W. (1955) 'Emotional and intellectual consequences of psychologic deprivation in infancy; a re-evaluation', in Hoch, P. and Zubin, J. (eds) *Psychopathology of Childhood* (New York: Grune). *14*

GLUECK, S. and GLUECK, E. (1956) *Physique and Delinquency* (New York: Harper Row). *10, 40*

HADDON, F. H. and LYTTON, H. (1968) 'Teaching approach and the development of divergent thinking abilities in primary school children', *British Journal of Educational Psychology* **38**, 2. *143*

HADDON, F. H. and LYTTON, H. (1971) 'Primary education and divergent thinking abilities — four years on', *British Journal of Educational Psychology* **41**, 2. *143*

HALL, C. and LINDZEY, G. (1970) *Theories of Personality* (New York: Wiley). *48, 166*

HARE, R. D. (1970) *Psychopathy; Theory and Research* (New York: Wiley. *159*

HARGREAVES, D. (1967) *Social Relations in a Secondary School* (London: Routledge and Kegan Paul). *42*

HARLOW, H. F. and HARLOW, M. H. (1962) 'Social deprivation in monkeys', *Scientific American* November. *16-17*

HARLOW, H. F. and HARLOW, M. H. (1966) 'Learning to love', *American Scientist* **54**, 3. *17*

HARTSHORNE, H. and MAY, M. (1928) *Studies in the Nature of Character* (New York: Macmillan). *90*

HESS, E. H. (1970) 'The ethological approach to socialisation', in Hoppe, R., Milton, G., and Simmel, E. (eds) *Early Experiences and the Processes of Socialisation* (New York: Academic Press). *20*

HINKLE, D. (1965) *The Change of Personal Constructs from the Viewpoint of a Theory of Implications* Unpublished Ph.D. thesis, Ohio State University. *84*

HUDSON, L. (1966) *Contrary Imaginations* (Harmondsworth: Pelican). *141, 143*

JAKUBCZAK, F. and WALTERS, R. (1959) 'Suggestibility as dependency behaviour', *Journal of Abnormal Social Psychology* **59**. *131*

JUNG, C. G. (1953-) *Collected Works* (Princeton: Princeton University Press). *63-6, 70-2, 99, 142*

KAGAN, J. (1966) 'Developmental studies in reflection and analysis', in Kidd, A. and Rivoire, J. (eds) *Perceptual Development in Children* (London: University of London Press). *152-4, 158*

KAGAN, J., SONTAG, L., BAKER, C., and NELSON, U. (1958) 'Personality and I.Q. change', *Journal of Abstract Social Psychology* **56**. *139*

KELLY, G. (1955) *The Psychology of Personal Constructs* 2 Vols (New York: Norton). *78-86*

KELVIN, P. (1970) *The Bases of Social Behaviour* (London: Holt, Rinehart and Winston). *92, 115*

KELVIN, P., LUCAS, C., and OJHA, A. (1965) 'The relation between personality, mental health, and educational performance in university students', *British Journal of Social Clinical Psychology* **4**. *105*

KOCH, H. (1956) 'Sissiness and tomboyishness in relation to sibling characteristics', *Journal of General Psychology* **88**. *27*

LACEY, C. (1970) *Hightown Grammar* (Manchester: Manchester University Press). *42*

LAING, R. D. and ESTERSON, A. (1964) *Sanity, Madness and the Family* (London: Tavistock). *162*

LEITH, G. and TROWN, E. A. (1970) 'The influence of personality and task conditions on learning and transfer', *Progress in Learning and Educational Techniques* **7**. *107*

LEWIN, K. (1935) *A Dynamic Theory of Personality* (New York: McGraw Hill). *87-96*

LEWIN, K. (1942) 'The relative effectiveness of a lecture method and a method of group decision for changing food habits', *Committee on Food Habits*. National Research Council. *92*

LEWIN, K., LIPPITT, R., and WHITE, R. (1939) 'Patterns of aggressive behaviour in experimentally created "social climates"', *Journal of Social Psychology* **10**. *93*

LEWIS, M. (1972) 'State as an infant-environment interaction; an analysis of mother–infant behaviour as a function of sex', *Merrill-Palmer Quarterly in Behavioural Development* **18**. *26*

LOVITT, T. (1970) 'Behaviour modification: the current scene', *Exceptional Children* **37**. *135*

LOWE, G. R. (1969) *Personal Relationships in Psychological Disorders* (Harmondsworth: Penguin). *162*

LYNN, R. (1971) *An Introduction to the Study of Personality* (London: Macmillan). *106, 108*

MAHER, B. A. (1970) *Principles of Psychopathology* (New York: McGraw Hill). *161, 167*

MARSTON, N. and SCOTT, D. (1970) 'Inconsequence as a primary type of behaviour disturbance in children', *British Journal of Educational Psychology* **40**, 1. *158*

MASLOW, A. H. (1970) *Motivation and Personality* (New York: Harper Row). *70-2, 85, 95, 101, 123*

MCCANDLESS, B. (1969) *Children; Behaviour and Development.* (London: Holt, Rinehart and Winston). *18, 140, 158*

MCDONALD, L. (1968) *Social Class and Delinquency* (London: Faber). *18*

MCKELLAR, P. (1957) *Imagination and Thinking* (London: Cohen and West). *143*

MCLELLAND, D. C. (1961) *The Achieving Society* (Princeton: Van Nostrand). *95-6*

MEAD, M. (1935) *Sex and Temperament in Three Primitive Societies* (New York: Morrow). *18*

MEHRABIAN, A. (1969) 'Measures of achieving tendency', *Educational Psychological Measurement* **29**. *95*

MILGRAM, S. (1974) *Obedience to Authority; an Experimental Overview* (London: Tavistock). *91*

MUSSEN, P. H., CONGER, J., and KAGAN, J. (1974) *Child Development and Personality* (New York: Harper Row). *6, 166*

NEWMAN, H., FREEMAN, F., and HOLZINGER, K. (1937) *Twins; a Study of Heredity and Environment* (Chicago: University of Chicago Press). *8*

OLIVER, R. A. and BUTCHER, H. J. (1968) 'Teachers' attitudes to education', *British Journal of Educational Psychology* **38**, 1. *121*

OSGOOD, C. E., SUCI, G., and TANNENBAUM, P. (1957) *The*

Measurement of Meaning (Urbana, Ill.: University of Illinois Press). *78, 116*

PARNELL, R. W. (1958) *Behaviour and Physique* (London: Arnold). *10*

POTEET, J. A. (1974) *Behaviour Modification* (London: University of London Press). *134*

PRICE, W. and WHATMORE, P. (1967) 'Behaviour disorders and pattern of crime among XYY males identified at a maximum security hospital', *British Medical Journal* **1**. *7*

RAVENETTE, A. (1975) 'Grid techniques for children', *Journal of Child Psychology and Psychiatry* **16**. *84*

RIDING, R. J. (1977) *School Learning: Mechanisms and Processes* (London: Open Books). *124*

ROBERTSON, J. (1962) 'Mothering as an influence in early development.' *Psychoanalytical Studies of the Child*, **17**. *15*

ROE, A. (1953) 'A psychological study of eminent psychologists and anthropologists, and a comparison with biological and physical scientists', *Psychological Monograms* **67**, 2. *140*

ROGERS, C. R. (1957) 'The necessary and sufficient conditions of therapeutic personality change', *Journal of Consulting Psychology* **21**. *76-7, 131*

ROGERS, C. R. (1961) *On Becoming a Person* (Boston: Houghton Mifflin). *72-7, 86, 101, 105, 142, 164, 165*

ROSEN, B. C. and D'ANDRADE, R. G. (1959) 'The psychosocial origin of achievement motivation', *Sociometry* **22**. *96*

ROSENBERG, M. (1965) *Society and the Adolescent Self-Image* (Princeton, New Jersey: Princeton University Press). *34*

ROSENTHAL, R. and JACOBSON, L. (1968) *Pygmalion in the Classroom* (New York: Holt, Rinehart and Winston). *81*

RUSHTON, J. (1966) 'The relationship between personality characteristics and scholastic success in eleven-year-old children', *British Journal of Educational Psychology* **36**, 2. *113*

RYANS, D. G. (1960) *Characteristics of Teachers* (Washington D.C.: American Council on Education). *121*

RYLE, A. (1969) *Student Casualties* (Harmondsworth: Allen Lane). *163*

SEARS, R., MACCOBY, E., and LEVIN, H. (1957) *Patterns of Child Rearing* (Evanston, Illinois: Row Peterson). *15*

SHELDON, W. H. (1954) *Atlas of Men.* (New York: Harper). *9-10*

SHELDON, W. H., LEWIS, N., and TENNEY, A. (1969) 'Psychotic patterns and physical constitution', in Sankar, D. (ed.) *Schizophrenia, Current Concepts and Research* (New York: PJD Publications). *10*

SHIELDS, J. (1962) *Monozygotic Twins* (Oxford: Oxford University Press). *8*

SKINNER, B. F. (1972) *Beyond Freedom and Dignity* (London: Jonathan Cape). *125-9, 130, 134, 136-7*

SMITH, P. K. (1974) Ethological methods, in Foss, B. (ed.) *New Perspectives in Child Development* (Harmondsworth: Penguin). *26*

STEWART, M. (1970) Hyperactive children. *Scientific American* April. *157-8*

TAYLOR, C. and HOLLAND, J. (1964) 'Predictors of creative performance', in Taylor, C. (ed.) *Creativity, Progress and Potential* (New York: McGraw Hill). *141*

TERMAN, L. and ODEN, M. (1947) *Genetic Studies of Genius IV* (Stanford, California: California University Press). *139-40*

TEYLER, T. J. (1975) *A Primer of Psychobiology* (San Francisco: Freeman). *22*

THARP, R. and WETZEL, R. (1969) *Behaviour Modification in the Natural Environment* (London: Academic Press). *135*

THOMAS, A., CHESS, S., and BIRCH, H. (1970) 'The origin of personality', *Scientific American* August. *11-13*

TROWN, E. A. and LEITH, G. (1975) 'Decision rules for teaching strategies in the primary school: personality-treatment interactions', *British Journal of Educational Psychology* **45**, 2. *105*

UNDERWOOD REPORT (1955) *Report of the Committee on Maladjusted Children* (London: HMSO). *155-7*

VALENTINE, C. W. (1956) *The Normal Child and some of his Abnormalities* (Harmondsworth: Pelican). *24, 25*

VERNON, P. E. (1975) Personality, in Eysenck, H. J., Arnold, W. and Meili, R. (eds) *Encyclopedia of Psychology Vol. 2* (London: Collins/Fontana). *3*

WANKOWSKI, J. (1970) *Personality Dimensions of Students and some Educational Implications of Eysenck's Theory of Extraversion and Neuroticism* (Birmingham: University of Birmingham Research Report). *108*

WATSON, J. B. and RAYNER, R. (1919) 'Conditioned emotional reactions', *Journal of Experimental Psychology* **3**. *124-5*

WHEELER, H. (ed.) (1973) *Beyond the Punitive Society* (London: Wildwood House). *136*

WHITE, R. and LIPPITT, R. (1960) 'Leader behaviour and member reaction in three social climates'. In Cartwright, D. and Zander, A. (eds) *Group Dynamics: Research and Theory* (New York: Harper Row). *93*

WILLIAMS, J. M. (1961) 'Children who break down in foster homes', *Journal of Child Psychology and Psychiatry* **2**. *15*

WISEMAN, S. and START, K. B. (1965) 'A follow-up of teachers five years after completing their training', *British Journal of Educational Psychology* **35**, 3. *122*

WITKIN, H. A. (1959) 'The perception of the upright', *Scientific American* February. *147-54*

WITKIN, H. A. (1965) 'Psychological differentiation and forms of pathology', *Journal of Abstract Psychology* **70**. *150*

WITKIN, H. A., LEWIS, H., HERTZMAN, M., MACHOVER, K., MEISSNER, P., and WAPNER, S. (1954) *Personality Through Perception* (New York: Harper Row). *148*

Subject index